Plaited
PATCHWORK

SHARI COLE

Plate 1. "Colourdance I – Hide and Seek," 49" x 44". This diagonal plait of dye-painted ripped strips is applied directly to a painted backing, with no batting used. It departs from its source, the mat woven with a planned color layout, in that strands change color unpredictably, and holes cut in strands reveal unexpected colors. Traditional quilt blocks, such as Four- and Nine-Patch, appear randomly at intersections, and insertions of new color into cutouts reintroduce some control. Machine quilting stabilizes the front and lays a thin colored grid over the backing, which also has holes cut and colored thread tassels.

↗laited
PATCHWORK

SHARI COLE

American Quilter's Society

P. O. Box 3290 • Paducah, KY 42002-3290

Located in Paducah, Kentucky, the American Quilter's Society (AQS), is dedicated to promoting the accomplishments of today's quilters. Through its publications and events, AQS strives to honor today's quiltmakers and their work – and inspire future creativity and innovation in quiltmaking.

DEDICATION

To my husband, photographer,
and co-conspirator in adventure,
Don Cole,
without whose support,
encouragement,
and occasional push off the deep end
I would be doing something much more ordinary.

Photography by Don Cole

Library of Congress Cataloging-in-Publication Data

Cole, Shari.
    Plaited patchwork / Shari Cole.
       p. cm.
    Includes bibliographical references.
    ISBN 0-89145-847-6
    1. Patchwork--Polynesia. 2. Quilting--Polynesia. 3. Braid-
-Polynesia. I. Title.
    TT835.C646 1995
    746.46--dc20   95-38422
                                                           CIP

Additional copies of this book may be ordered from: American Quilter's Society, P.O. Box 3290, Paducah, KY 42002-3290 @ $19.95. Add $2.00 for postage & handling.

Copyright: 1995, Shari Cole.

Printed by IMAGE GRAPHICS, INC., Paducah, Kentucky

ACKNOWLEDGMENTS

First I acknowledge the tufunga fai lalanga, the weavers of ancient times, and those who grow from their roots.

For my first skills in plaiting, quilting, and garment making, I thank the women named and unnamed who so generously taught and encouraged me:

My grandmother, Mary Chance, quiltmaker, and my aunt, Evelyn Chance, dressmaker, who set the example of recreation through creative work.

Mrs. Sunia of Fagatogo, American Samoa, for my first lalanga lessons.

Tina Wirihana of Waiariki Polytech, Rotorua, New Zealand, for the addition of Maori raranga techniques to my island foundations.

Mechtild Prangnell, for a sound introduction to European basketry.

The Samoan, Niuean, and Tongan weavers who shared their expertise and time in the years of my craft and writing apprenticeships for Tusitala magazine and other publications.

Carolyn Colledge, who kept up my enthusiasm for quiltmaking, and accepted my strange ways of going about it.

Alison Gray, whose own approach to plaited fabric, so different from mine, pushed me to seek new directions.

For the extension of lalanga skills and a real understanding of basic moves previously done by rote, the elder teachers of Niue and Tokelau, especially:

Vitolia Kulatea, project field organizer, translator, and coresearcher of the Niue craft recording project.

Niuean teachers Melemoka Siavale, Tupekula Tauetau, Mesulama Tangelagi, Pepa Tuaga, Meleaisa Ikitoemata, and Kelena Kulatea, whose project demonstrations most influenced the work in this book.

Members of the Aualuma (women's organization) of Atafu, Tokelau, for patient demonstration and hospitable sharing of their lives.

Also those members of the Aualuma of Nukunonu who made time to teach for the Tokelau craft project during a busy season.

For the professional help, advice, and encouragement without which I would not have perservered as a teacher, writer, and artist:

Helen Kelley, for years of friendship and support, and also Mary Coyne Penders and Nancy Crow who, like Helen, added to their interest the confidence to hire me for their faculties.

Other quilting colleagues a step above me – the tufunga of the West – whose achievements are stars to reach for.

Conference organizers in New Zealand and America, Waiariki and Wanganui Polytechs, editors, and sponsors who have accepted my work and services – and most particularly the students, readers, and viewers who support us all.

A special thanks to Edith Ryan and the Queen Elizabeth II Arts Council of New Zealand for grants which made some overseas lectures and courses of study possible.

For the use of her work as illustration, and her enthusiastic approach to plaited patchwork, Anne Pluck of Wanganui.

For kindly modeling the garments for illustrations: Elizabeth Miles, Penelope Barker, and Amber Pool. "Sunset of the Weaver Wizards" photo supplied by Fairfield Processing Corporation.

And thanks to the American Quilter's Society, their editors and staff, for their faith that this book is a worthwhile undertaking, and all their work to bring it to production.

CONTENTS

How to Use This Book

Pacific plaiting is an entire field, just as quiltmaking is an entire field. The set of skills involved takes years to master. In this book we dip our fingers into the different elements of plaiting and plaited patchwork. Skills are cumulative, right through this book.

Chapter One surveys the field. Read it first and refer to it as we come to each element later. Read the basic strand construction methods in Chapter Two, and use this for reference in later work. Then work through the exercises and projects in each chapter following. You won't understand later directions until your hands have been through the early motions.

Have patience with the first easy projects. They get harder. They get very hard. You are condensing seven years of my studies into the time it takes you to work through this book. Instructions are precise at first, but gradually I give you scope to insert your own ideas. By the time we finish, your work will have more of you in it than of me. You will have tried my working methods and altered them to your own preferences.

In Chapter One we begin the "Flying Time" exercises and thoughts. You don't need them to travel in a straight line through the book. They are creative playtime designed to broaden your approach – to play with some aspect of the chapter in an open way.

Have patience also with the frequent instruction to refer to other photos and diagrams. Keep a stack of bookmarks handy. Keep your own exercises and projects where you can see them and remember what you did.

Above all, pursue the knowledge for your own enjoyment and enhancement. A project is not the end in itself, but a souvenir of your journey.

PRONOUNCING POLYNESIAN WORDS

In simple terms, the vowels are similar to those in Spanish and Latin. Every vowel is sounded and every syllable ends with a vowel sound. Consonants are similar to those in English, except the "ng," and "g" by itself are pronounced as in "song."

Accents usually fall on the next-to-last syllable of a word, but the meaning of a compound word, or borrowing from another language, sometimes changes this. Pronounce lalanga as lah-lahng´-ah, and ala as ah´-lah, without really saying the h.

GLOSSARY OF A FEW TERMS

Ala – in diagonal plaiting, a section worked across the mat as one unit of working (hala, ara)

Allowances:

Takeup allowance – extra strand length required for the journey over and under other strands, for thickness

Expansion allowance – the amount by which a mat grows wider than the simple sum of strand widths, during weaving

Safety allowance – extra strand length to avoid running out due to variations in thickness and tension of weaving

Seam allowance, joining allowance – at ends of strands this allows addition of bindings, sashes, or other strands

Commencement corner – lower left corner of a mat, where set-up and weaving start, especially with reference to diagonal corner starts

Commencement edge – edge of the mat closest to the weaver, where work starts

Lalanga – the Polynesian term for weaving without looms, by picking up and laying down strands (lalaga, raranga)

Left-pointer (sinistral) – strand pointing diagonally away and to the left of the weaver

Right-pointer (dextral) – strand pointing diagonally away and to the right of the weaver

Working row, Working strands – the row immediately involved in the weaving, and the strands being raised and lowered *across* this row

Plate 2. Sunset of the Weaver Wizards. In the cool of the Pacific sunset, island women again take up their weaving, plaiting subtle patterns in ancient material of pandanus and coconut leaf. As the day ends in darkness, the old women lie down to sleep. We who rise in the dawn to prepare the new strands will remember them in our weaving.

As a child I loved stories about the South Pacific, and how people there once made everything they needed from the restricted range of natural materials on their islands. As a young mother, I was privileged to live for nine years in American Samoa, and to learn some of those admired skills. Later still, I visited other Pacific islands as feature writer for a regional airline magazine. My favorite interviews were with craftspeople, and customary practices were often the subject of articles.

The major items of women's manufacture – woven mats and patterned tapa cloth – I saw in a social role, much in common with that of quilts in nineteenth century America. Women often worked on them in groups. Skill in design and execution brought respect. Here women's craft products served as gifts of prestige for important occasions, to a much greater degree than in western countries. They represented the good will, generosity, and wealth of extended families. In the eastern islands, I soon discovered, these gifts had long ago changed from mats and tapa to quilt-like bedcovers – tivaevae. The western quilt tradition had been converted to Polynesian forms and purposes.

By this time I had become a quilter, like my grandmother before me. It was a time when people everywhere were looking back at cultural traditions and skills nearly lost in the onrush of modern life. While Samoan and Tongan women took interest in quilting as a new craft from outside, they put tapa and weaving first, as their cultural identity. As a quilter in Samoa I found it natural to use tapa motifs in my appliqué, and tapa print fabrics in piecework – a drawing together of personal experiences.

Quilts designed from mat weaving and basketry, however, required a leap – a breaking of European quilt rules. One day the simple geometry of mats – the squares, rectangles, and diamonds – spoke to me. The pieced and quilted bedcovers of the north touched the plaited mats of the south, and their fibers intermeshed. My concept of quilts expanded.

Stepping outside of assumptions and definitions is the heart of creativity. When we can see that categories – basket, mat, quilt, garment – are convenient shorthand labels rather than boxes for unrelated things, we can flow from one art to another, and from one culture to another.

So it is with learning. We take something out, and we put something back in. We extend our traditions by exchanging them. We multiply our knowledge by playing with its components. Our teachers are amplified in the experiments and discoveries of their students.

Each of us who learns, develops the idea, and passes it on to others, is like the increase-point of a circular mat. Strands from the past converge and fold around the new strand. Old and new bend and flow away as the mat grows larger. New patterns emerge, but the center remains.

Introductory Photos

Plate 3. Fine mats delicately woven from a special variety of pandanus form the highest medium of exchange in Samoa. Important ceremonies, such as the investiture of high titles, require gifts of many such mats, presented by strict protocol. Vaimoso, Western Samoa, 1984.

Plate 4. To honor dignitaries and guests, the reviewing stand is roofed with mats typically used for seating guests. Mats embroidered with yarn pictures in long stitch decorate the pavilion. Sixteenth Independence celebration, Mulinu'u, Western Samoa, 1978.

Plate 5. The labor of many hands, the power to command that labor, and the skill to do the work combine in the prestige of mats as gifts. Pacific island weavers possess the knowledge of cultivation, processing, and forming the material into articles of beauty. First comes the work, then the pleasure of weaving. Nukunonu atoll, Tokelau, is known for its fine pandanus grove and the skill of its weavers, 1989.

Plate 6. Mats, roof thatch, and coconut house blinds are still part of everyday life, though not so much as a few years ago. Here pandanus leaf cures in the sun in the seaside village of Papa, Savaii, Western Samoa, 1978.

Chapter One
MOTHERS OF INVENTION

BACKGROUND

The idea of weaving is so old and so universal that we must credit it to a myriad of clever people through the ages who experienced the great "Aha!" Whether their necessity was a roof for shelter, a basket for more fruit than they could eat, or a garment against rain and cold, these ancient inventors saw that they could interlace short fibrous elements to fabricate the needed shape.

In lands where wooly animals, silkworms, or cotton grew, the idea led to cloth as we know it. Elsewhere, especially in the rainy tropics, the mothers of invention adapted the techniques and materials of basket weaving to produce bedding and clothing. Firm, even after special processing, these materials hold their places without the aid of looms. In these weaving techniques, called plaiting, there is neither warp nor weft. All strands are equal, and held in place by the weaving itself or by temporary unsplit tags. Polynesian women of the South Pacific islands call their system of plaiting *lalanga*.

Invented in response to necessity, lalanga became "unnecessarily beautiful" – a term anthropologists have used for artifacts which go beyond the requirements of function to aesthetic appeal. There is something in human nature that seeks beauty and harmony – a spirit of play. From ancient days until now, Polynesian women have played with lalanga design.

When the obvious door is closed, we look for others we wouldn't have tried if it were open. On small islands of limited mineral and vegetable resources the door to varied and permanent color was closed. Polynesian women turned to design elements inherent in the process of lalanga.

ELEMENTS IN PACIFIC PLAITING
TEXTURE

The structure of plaiting produces light and shadow much as quilting does. Shapes repeat in an allover pattern. Because strands are split along the grain of leaves, their widths vary slightly (Plate 7).

Because the weaver's hands control the tension, it varies. Thus the nature of plaiting gives us two options as craftspeople – both satisfying. We can strive for technical perfection, lines and angles as regular as possible. Or we can enjoy the subtle random variations of size, shape, angle, and line unified by the allover weave (Plate 8).

SHAPE

The repeated shapes of lalanga, mostly squares, reflect the over and under alternations of strands. Thus we can change squares to rectangles by skipping strands. Our choices are:

•Checkerwork – over one, under one – which gives squares and a physically strong mat.

•Twill – a repeated pattern of skips – for example, over two, under three – which creates rectangles and rhythmic lines (Plate 9).

•Twill medallions – self-contained sets of varied overs and unders surrounded by checkerwork – which produces a dominant group of rectangles, a similar effect to medallion quilts (Plate 10).

•Twill and checker combinations in repeating units – which gives an effect similar to repeated quilt blocks (Plate 11).

The repetition of related shapes creates

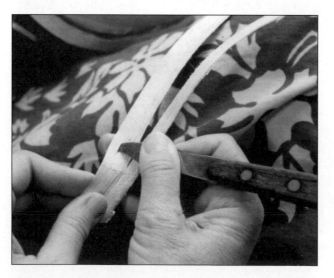

Plate 7. Weavers split strips of processed pandanus leaf into narrow strands by sliding a sharp instrument down the grain, as we would rip fabric on grain. The unsplit tag controls strands at the start of weaving.

Plate 8. A Samoan sleeping mat in ⅜" strands makes a texture study.

unity, the sense that a composition hangs together. The unity of plaited patchwork gives us freedom to use many diverse elements within it.

•Value Changes. Black and white photos in this chapter show the pattern features emphasized by light/medium/dark contrasts. Natural dyes in black and brown combine with the response of different types of pandanus to drying, boiling, and sunning. This gives a range of values. By understanding how a given strand will appear and disappear throughout the weave, we create pattern from light, medi-

Plate 10. Traditional Niuean twill medallion handbags by teacher and student: Large bag, author's commission to Melemoka Siavale; small bag, author's learning project.

Plate 9. Traditional twill work in split coconut frond: Niuean basket, gift of Vitolia Kulatea; Tokelauan food serving mat, gift of the aualuma (women's organization) of Atafu, Tokelau.

Plate 11. Detail of repeat twill mat purchased from a Tongan dealer, 1966.

um, and dark – much as we create pattern in quilt blocks.

When strands vary in value along their lengths we have interesting surprises. Plate 12 compares two Tokelauan double-weave checkerwork mats. Both have formal value layouts. The lighter mat above is more precise. Its value layout balances left and right, creating a regular pattern.

In the lower mat, variations in strand width, tension, and the shading of individual strands create an irregular play of shape, line, and value. The layout repeats but does not balance left and right exactly. The pair of cream strands running from the lower left to the upper right corner is replaced on the lower right to upper left axis by a pair of tan strands. Compare this to cream and tan in the general layout.

Like two quilts of different intentions, the mats contrast. One has a comfortable stability and predictability, the other an intriguing sense of motion (Plate 12).

•Set. The squares of mats in Plate 12 appear as fat diamonds. Their apparent shape is changed by being stood on its ear – set on point

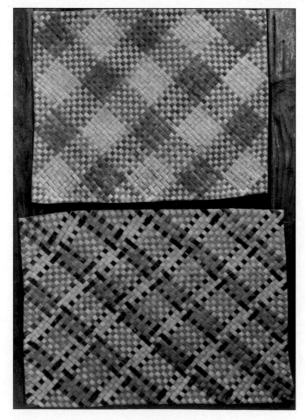

Plate 12.

as quilters say. Many Polynesian mats and baskets use this diagonal weave.

Is the ever-available coconut frond the historical reason for this? Split a frond in half down the main rib, turn one half end for end, and lay it on top of the first half with main ribs together. You have a firm starting edge for weaving. Half the leaflets point to the left and half to the right, ready for interlacing. All leaflets are controlled by the main rib – no setting up or wandering off course. You can quickly produce roof thatch, floor coverings, food trays, and baskets (Plate 9, Plate 13, and Plate 14).

But coconut leaflets are short. They shrink and lose strength as they dry. Pandanus leaves are durable, long, and easy to split uniformly. However, they require processing before use.

Did the mothers of invention start with coconut fronds and then replace them with superior materials laid out to repeat the familiar form? Or was it design – the quest for unnecessary beauty – that led them to set horizontal weave on point?

Whichever way it happened, they opened new doors for us. Right angle set (90˚) is common, but we can change that to produce long diamonds and parallelograms (Plate 15).

•Strand Width. We can change shapes also by changing widths of strands, making various rectangles. We can weave narrow through wide or arbitrarily mix widths. With practice, we can create optical illusions. Plate 16 resulted from playtime with scissors, typing paper, and a too-dark photocopy.

Plate 13. Residents of Atafu, Tokelau, work communally. This group splits coconut frond and plaits food baskets and trays, while others prepare traditional food and the earth oven in which to cook it, 1988.

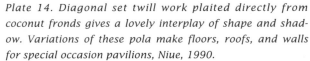

Plate 14. Diagonal set twill work plaited directly from coconut fronds gives a lovely interplay of shape and shadow. Variations of these pola make floors, roofs, and walls for special occasion pavilions, Niue, 1990.

MOTHERING NEW INVENTIONS

•Color. The color door closed in ancient times now stands open. In the islands, purists and tourists prefer the "authentic" shades of brown, black, and cream. Island women oblige them when they weave for sale and to represent tradition. When they weave for themselves, out come dyes from the store. Fuchsia, electric blue, and purple enliven the natural cream. Old pat-

Plate 15. Author's experiment with pandanus set at a nontraditional angle, with a curved commencement edge and random strand values.

Plate 17. Tokelauan men's malo – fringe-kilts for formal occasions – employ traditional patterns inlaid over the structural weave during construction. Modern dyes encourage evolution of pattern in color. Nukunonu, Tokelau, 1989.

Plate 16.

Plate 18. Dyed strands in the original layout produce plaid-like patterns in fancy mats. Tokelauan weavers use slanted wooden weaving boards to support the work at an efficient angle for working seated on the floor mats.

terns gain new excitement. Weavers who have moved to New Zealand, far from pandanus supplies, use colored plastic packing strips for sturdy tote bags. The canvas of daily life now reflects the colorful canvas of nature (Plate 17 and Plate 18).

In plaiting cloth we use color continually, so let's review some color terms:

• Hue – the name of the color (red, orange, blue-green)

• Complementary color – opposites on the color wheel (blue and orange, for example)

• Analogous color – next to one another on the color wheel (red, red-violet, violet)

• Value – dark, medium, light

• Shade – darker than the parent hue

• Tint – lighter than the parent hue

• Intensity (saturation) – how pure the color is (high intensity) or how gray it is (low intensity). Tone, a *grayed* version of a color, should not be confused with shade or tint.

You will find that plaiting color, breaking it up into small shapes, also changes our perception of it. Surprise lies in wait for us as we play with invention.

FLYING TIME

Before you walk onward on our carefully mapped path, take off on a tangent. View the subject from a slant. Try your wings on these flying exercises for which there are no "right" answers. The higher a flight of fancy, the farther the horizon retreats. Your world grows wider.

• 1. Find a magazine picture you like. Slice it into strips but leave one edge joined like the pandanus strips on unsplit tags. This keeps the picture in order.

• 2. Slice a sheet of white paper and a sheet of black paper into separate strips.

• 3. Weave the white strips through the sliced picture, checkerboard fashion. What do you see? Do the colors change? Can your eye still put the picture back together?

• 4. Remove the white strips and substitute the black strips. Do colors change? Does mood change?

Play with the idea. How can you change the exercise? Are there rules about this? Who makes the rules?

Chapter Two

A New Net Goes Fishing

Your quilt and garment-making traditions come from centuries of dependence on materials made by others. In contrast, Pacific island women are less than a century and a half (some only a few years) from total dependence upon themselves for cultivating materials, gathering, and making everything in their lives. Those now middle aged grew up making substantial portions of their own household goods.

There is power in knowing a craft from its source in nature to the fine points of finishing. Few of us experience this in our work with fabric, but we are compensated by an immense range of choice.

We have color and print in cloth. We have threads that sparkle and trinkets that shine. We have specialist tools and machines. And we have *time* borrowed from cultivation and processing that is transferred to design and elaboration.

Nevertheless, for quilts and garments plaited from this new medium of cloth, we too must process materials. We wash and iron fabrics to prevent shrinkage and color bleeding. Like the mat weavers, we make strands from our cloth. What type of strands? How shall we make them? What problems and opportunities will we encounter in using them?

Cloth strands differ from pandanus strands in character and behavior. They are limp and don't hold their space in the weaving. However, we can pin and sew them into positions not suitable for pandanus. Cloth frays along cut edges, but pandanus cracks in dry air when folded too many times. Mats plaited of cloth drape well, and can be stitched and cut to new shapes. Finally, through color, print, and texture, cloth sets a mood. Cheerful country and opulent Oriental await our choice.

DIFFERENT STRANDS FOR DIFFERENT REASONS

•Strips. The simplest strips are cut on grain,

Plate 19.

with edges left raw. For practice mats you need do no more. For a soft fringed effect in a permanent composition, pull threads from the long edges (Plate 19).

How will you use raw-edge weavings? Stitching, perhaps hand or machine embroidery, can stabilize their edges and enhance the design.

•Ribbons. These come in premeasured widths with nonfraying edges. You can trim their ends to decorative points and fray-proof them. Their moods are dainty, luxurious, or festive. You need more pins to hold these slippery strands while plaiting (Plate 20).

Plate 20.

Plate 20 shows a springtime composition of pastel ribbons in various textures, hues, and widths. Irregular cross-stitch in fine Kreinik metallic glitter braid secures the plait to its wooden form.

•Strips with Ironed-over Edges. These folded-edge strands make instant patchwork as we weave. You can prepare them in two ways:

1. For slightly variable width, cut strips ½" wider than the finished strand. Place each strip face down on the ironing board. Fold ¼" seam allowance on each side at the *beginning of the strip*, and secure the end to the board with two pins. With both hands turn the same seam allowance a few inches from the pins and pull. The seam allowances will curl into place (Plate 21).

As in Plate 22, hold the turned strip down firmly with one hand, keeping the tension. With the other hand lower the iron. A patting motion coaxes edges to roll evenly.

Set the iron for a temperature that makes a crease but will not scorch if the iron is left down for a few seconds. Set the iron on the pressed area for the weight. Again move both hands farther along the strip. Turn seam allowances and pull. Hold and press as before. Repeat until either the strip or the ironing board runs out.

You will learn how far ahead to turn edges. I find that four to six inches, the width of my iron, is the maximum for cotton cloth cut on the cross grain. Cotton cut on the lengthwise grain rolls more easily when tensioned. The full length of the iron works here.

2. Method 1 suits most purposes. Small variations average out, and slight irregularities suit the nature of plaiting. However, when precise measurements count, as in making uniform blocks for joining, iron strips over a guide of thin card. Add ¾" for seam allowance, as narrow turns are difficult to fold.

Lay the cloth strip face down with the guide

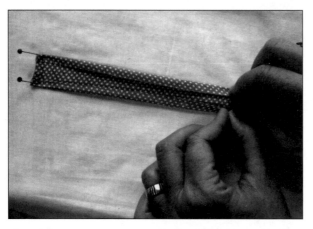

Plate 21.

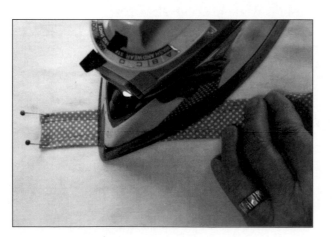

Plate 22.

Plate 23.

on top of it. With fingers and thumb fold up the seam allowances at the beginning of the strip. Press these, then let the iron hold the card and folded cloth as you run your fingers and thumb just ahead of the advancing iron. Glide the iron instead of patting (Plate 23).

Work from the right-hand end of the strip if you are right-handed. When you run out of card, push it ahead to the next section. If necessary, let the iron sit on creases as the card is pulled forward.

You will find that thin material shows shadows of seams, just as in conventional piecework. Choose opaque fabric for light colors.

STORING PREPARED STRIPS

You want your ironed strips to stay creased. Island weavers want their processed strips to stay flat. The same device solves both problems – the flat coil called masina, the moon. Ribbons and fringed strips are also stored conveniently this way.

Use a spool, or two fingers, for the core of your moon coil. Roll the ironed strips around this core with *seam allowances facing the outside* of the coil. Edges remain folded because they have to travel farther than the center of the strip to complete the circle. This places tension on them.

Roll a separate coil for each value or color. As each strip is ironed, add it to the coil before it uncurls. Secure the coils with pins or a tie through the center hole. Plate 24 shows moon coils of pandanus and cloth tied this way.

DOUBLETHINK: FABRIC TUBES

Pandanus mats are reversible. For reversible fabric projects we machine sew tubes with raw edges hidden inside.

Cut each cloth strip twice as wide as the finished strand, plus ½" seam allowance. A 1" wide tube strand needs a 2½" wide strip. A 1½" wide tube strand needs a 3½" strip.

Fold the strip in half along its length, wrong side out. Pin occasionally and stitch the long side and across one end. For a long tube, stitch both ends closed, but leave an opening for turning near the center of the long side. Press to set

Plate 24.

the stitches (Figure 1).

Turn the tube right side out and press it flat, with the seam down one side. Not easy, you say? These methods work for me.

A device called Fasturn® consists of a smooth metal pipe with a long wire corkscrew hook to insert through it. The sewn fabric tube is packed on the pipe wrong side out. By hooking the end of the fabric tube through the pipe, you draw it inside and out the other end, right side out.

These pipes come in sizes up to 2½" circumference, large enough for a fabric tube 1½" pressed flat. *Depending on fabric thickness*, you can turn well over a yard of tubing. You can double that length by turning through the center opening. Insert the pipe at the center and turn one end of the tube. Slip the pipe off the turned end. Insert the pipe into the remaining end and turn that (Plate 25).

Longer and larger tubes are turned with ingenuity. You need a pipe one or more yards

long. It *need not be hollow beyond the first few inches,* but must fit loosely inside your fabric tube. I use a bamboo rake handle. Yours might be plastic plumbing pipe or a cardboard tube from a roll of curtain fabric. Sand the end smooth and be sure the inside is clean.

You also need a ramrod that fits *loosely* into the pipe, such as a broom handle or wooden dowel. To reduce fabric abrasion, turn tubes through the center opening, rather than full length.

Follow the steps in Plates 25 through 28.

Insert the pipe into the fabric tube. Pack fabric on until you reach its sewn end. Pack as close to this end as possible.

Plate 26.

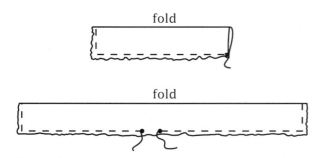
Figure 1.

Plate 25.

Plate 27.

Plate 28.

Push the ramrod into the fabric-covered end of the pipe.

This forces fabric into the pipe right side out.

Ease the *packed* fabric off the pipe and onto the ramrod, keeping pipe and ramrod *engaged.*

When the end of the ramrod, now covered with fabric, emerges from the packed fabric, remove the pipe (Plate 26).

Grasp the packed fabric and pull the ramrod out (Plate 27).

Pull on the turned end of the tube, while grasping the pack with the other hand. The fabric tube will continue to turn through the pack, as in Plate 28.

Square the corners of turned strands by teasing out with a pin. Flatten the tube and pin both corners to the ironing board, at left if you're right-handed, and with the seamed side away from you. Pull hard on the seam from farther down the tube, coaxing the tube to fold flat. Clamp it to the board with left thumb and fingers while applying the iron.

Weight the pressed area with the iron as you move toward the pins. Your left hand controls the fold as the iron follows. Pin both ends of the tube if needed to keep the tension on. This stretches the seam as well as flattening it (Plate 29).

FLYING TIME

Make a few of each kind of strip. Interweave and manipulate them without a particular goal. Explore their properties. Ask, "What if, and Why?" Start a log book of ideas and questions. When you think of one in future work, write or sketch it. Then return to the line you were pursuing. Reject no ideas. Later they may make sense.

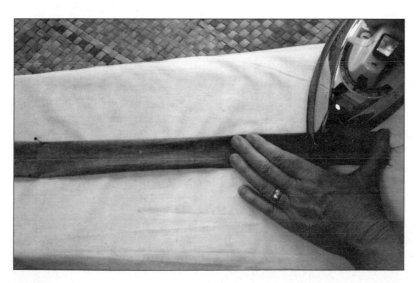

Plate 29.

Chapter Three
GOING THROUGH THE MOTIONS

LALANGA: THE DANCE OF THE HANDS

By now you've found that lacing strips over and under other strips using no particular technique is a clumsy business. Coordinating fingers and hands brings both speed and enjoyment of the plaiting motion. The motions and the simple equipment used with them solve several problems:

•Holding the woven sheet in place as you work.

•Opening rows of alternate vertical strands to admit horizontal strands.

•Holding the new horizontal in the row as you close it.

•Keeping rows, and the edges of woven sheets, straight.

For your practice samples use paper strips. Like pandanus, paper retains its shape and will crease. Let's begin with a checkerboard in dark and light, following Figures 2 – 3 and Plates 30 through 34.

You need:

•A square of cork or soft board that accepts pins. Corrugated cardboard or styrofoam will do for paper mats.

•Straight pins, glue, pencil, transparent ruler.

•Scissors – rotary cutter and board desirable.

•Paper in black, white, and medium gray.

Procedure:

1. Your weaving board has straight edges to help you keep the weave straight. Across the center of the board draw a horizontal line and a vertical line, crossing at the center point. These give additional reference lines.

Cut strips of black and gray paper ½" wide by about 8½" long, the width of standard typing paper. For convenience in starting your mats, cut ½" strips lengthwise on the white paper, leaving the first inch at the bottom uncut. See Figure 2.

Count 15 strips for this tag set and remove the extras. This is the set of *vertical strands* for your checkerboard.

2. Lay the tag set on the weaving board, tag edge close and parallel to the edge of the board nearest you. Pin the two bottom corners to the board. As in Figure 3, raise every second strand

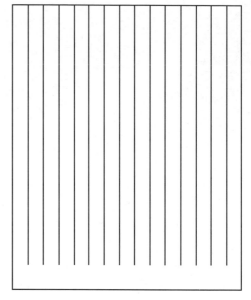

Figure 2.

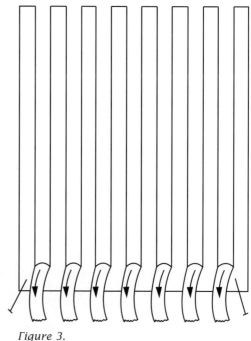

Figure 3.

to open the first row for a horizontal strand.

3. Lay in the first dark horizontal strand. Keep it parallel to the edge of the weaving board and the tag set. If you lowered the raised strands you would see the first row of checkers,

24

but this is not how we weave efficiently. The dark horizontal would tend to creep away from the commencement edge. Plate 30 shows where we are.

Plate 30.

4. Lower only two raised vertical strands, near the center. Your thumbs do this job easily, while your fingers hold the horizontal strand in place (Plate 31).

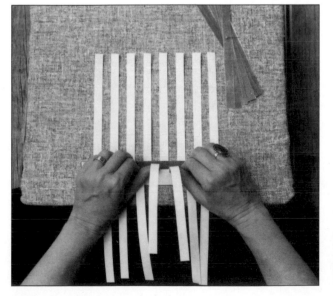

Plate 31.

5. To keep it there, raise the vertical strand between the two you just lowered. Your left hand steadies the horizontal strand (Plate 32).

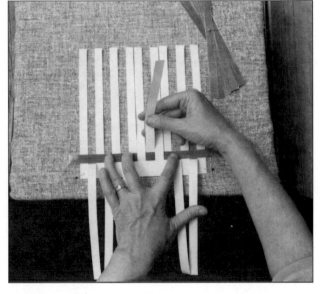

Plate 32.

6. Crease the vertical strand just raised (right thumb) while your fingers scoop up another strand from those originally down. Your left hand steadies the left end of the horizontal strand while your left thumb begins to lower another raised vertical (Plate 33).

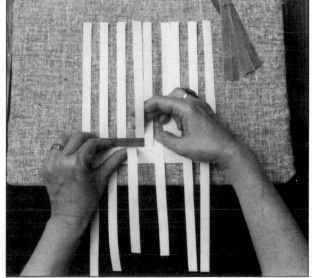

Plate 33.

7. Continue to lower the vertical strands originally raised and raise the vertical strands originally down. Crease each strand that you raise, so that it stays up and holds the horizontal strand firmly in place. In Plate 34 the left end of the row is finished. The hands are working together to raise and lower vertical strands, moving toward the right-hand end of the row. This opens a new row for horizontal strand 2.

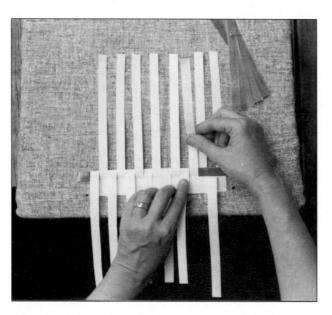

Plate 34.

Lay in horizontal strand 2 and repeat steps 3 through 7. It does not matter where in the row you begin step 3 or whether you work first to left or to right. A mix of starting points and directions from row to row helps keep the weave even. Your hands exchange jobs as you move in different directions. Work out what is comfortable and efficient to you. Thumbs and fingers can raise, crease, and lower strands in a coordinated and continuous motion. Pin the ends of some horizontal rows.

Add a total of 15 rows to your checkerboard mat. The sides will tend to spread as horizontal strands force vertical strands apart. To allow the bottom of the mat to expand slightly, *clip the connecting tag* in several places. It has served its purpose of controlling the start.

Save your sample mats for a pattern index. Figure 4 shows an easy edge finish.

Fold the overstroke strands at edges and top of the mat to the back. Glue them. Then trim the understroke strands (those that emerge from under the last row at edges and top) even with mat edges. Leave the tags at the commencement edge. Write the pattern on them. This checker pattern is "Verticals: 15 light, Horizontals: 15 dark."

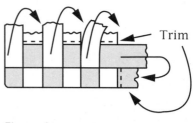

Trim

Figure 4.

THE VALUE OF PLAY

Your first visual clue to shape and the relationships among shapes is value. Let's play with some ways of organizing value placement in lalanga blocks. First we need a system of writing down the patterns so that we can remember them. Then we'll plait blocks and play perception and imagination games with them.

The terms light, medium, and dark can represent any color. We abbreviate them as L, M, D. For vertical strands we write Vrt, and horizontal strands, Hrz. A chart like the one below is easy to compare to an actual woven block. However, the abbreviated pattern to its right is quicker to write and read.

```
     D
     D
     D
     M
     M
     M        Block A    Vrt: 15L
     L                   Hrz: 3D, 3M, 3L, 3M, 3D
Hrz. L        Read Vertical directions left to right.
     L        Read Horizontal directions bottom to top.
     M        This is the order in which you lay out
     M        verticals and lay in horizontals.
     M
     D
     D
     D
   L L L L L L L L L L L L L L L
              Vrt.
```

26

Plate 35.

Plait and glue the charted block. Call it block A. Write the abbreviated pattern on its tags when you finish.

Check your finished block against block A, Plate 35. Fold the tags to the back, so that you see only the pattern. Pin the block to a wall and answer these questions while looking from a distance:

•What do you see? Checkers? Rows of dark squares? Diagonal rows of light squares? Crosses? Shaded horizontal bands?

•Does squinting or darkening the room change your perceptions?

•Which blends together more easily – the strong light/dark contrast or the lesser light and medium contrast?

•Does the block hang together or appear as two separate areas? Why?

•How did the layout cause the white band to form?

•What happens to the line dividing the white area from the light/medium checker area?

•Imagine this as the basis of a picture – a land, city, or seascape – to which you will later add detail. Which area is farthest away? Which is nearest? What might the picture be about?

Turn the block on its side so that the light band is vertical. How does your perception change? Notice how easily the solid band steals squares from its neighbors. Answer the questions above again. Do some answers change? How might the appearance of our everyday surroundings influence the "pictures" we see? Note that the dark checker band begins with two dark squares (first and third rows) while the medium checker band begins and ends with two light squares. How does this affect how you see the band?

Lastly, place the block on point. Squares become diamonds. Do you get a feeling of movement compared to the feeling of the block set square? On the square this block is formally balanced. Right mirrors left. Top mirrors bottom. Placing it on point complicates the balance. Right and left have the same amounts of light, medium, and dark but these do not mirror.

Think about this block layout. We balanced the horizontal values symmetrically from the center (eighth) row. Verticals are also symmetrical, and the same value. However, we chose different sets of values for verticals and for horizontals. Divide the block diagonally, corner to corner, with a line. Divide it diagonally again, into quarters. Two of them are the same. The other two match each other but not the first two (Plate 36).

Let's define the characteristics of the Type A Block Layout:

•The same uneven number of vertical and horizontal strands, for example, 9, 11, 17.

•Only one value for vertical strands – automatic symmetry.

•More than one value for horizontal strands.

•Horizontal strand values arranged symmetrically from the center. The number of strands in each value group need not be the

Plate 36.

same. We could use four dark and two medium, for example.

Let's proceed to the characteristics of the Type B Block Layout:

•More than one value for both vertical and horizontal strands.

•A different value set for verticals than for horizontals.

•Both vertical and horizontal values arranged symmetrically from the center.

Plait and glue this layout pattern. Check your block with B in Plate 35. Cut vertical strands as tag sets of five to avoid many pins.

```
        M
        M
        M
        M
        M         Vrt: 5D, 5L, 5D
        D
        D         Hrz: 5M, 5D, 5M
Hrz.    D
        D
        D
        M
        M
        M
        M
        M
          D D D D D L L L L L D D D D D
                        Vrt.
```

Again question what you see. Does this block look like an assembly of sub-blocks? What happens to the "edge" between the sub-block where dark crosses dark and the other sub-blocks touching it? Notice how light verticals overpower the medium horizontals but set up a conversation with the dark horizontals.

Turn the block on its side. Notice how light/medium sub-blocks lose their edges where light touches medium and medium touches dark in the sub-blocks on either side. If this block were the basis for a picture scape, what might it be?

Set Block B on point and compare it to block A on point. Divide it diagonally into quarters and identify the pairs of quarters. This block is balanced but not symmetrical in all directions.

Let's plait a Type C Block Layout, symmetrical in all directions:

•The same set of values for horizontal as for vertical strands.

•Both horizontals and verticals arranged symmetrically from the center, the same arrangement for both sets.

Plait this layout pattern and check it with block C in Plate 35. Vrt: 3D, 3M, 3L, 3M, 3D. Hrz: 3D, 3M, 3L, 3M, 3D. Study this block placed horizontally and vertically. Why do solid areas of light, medium, and dark form? Why are these solid areas not the same in the diagonally divided block? If you used an even number of strands for each value would that make the solid areas the same shape? Would the block itself still be symmetrical? The nature of checkerwork produces a block symmetrical only on the horizontal and vertical axes.

Note the effect of light rays across the center and a dark frame. This generally symmetrical effect works well on the square or on point.

Having produced maximum symmetry, let's move on to progressive shading. The Type D Block has:

•Vertical groups progressing in value from light to dark.

•Horizontal groups arranged symmetrically from the center, using two or more values. Plait this pattern layout and compare it to block D in Plate 35. Vrt: 5L, 5M, 5D. Hrz: 5D, 5M, 5D.

Since the western mind scans images from left to right, this block might suggest the coming of the day, or the advance of a force. By turning the block upside down you may find other interpretations. View it from far away and look for a lattice effect.

Now turn the block on its side, with the darkest areas at top. Imagine as many "pictures" as possible, close up and far away. Reverse the block, with darks at the bottom. What do you see now?

From my own experiences, I see a moonlit sea viewed from under a dark lattice gateway. In reverse position, I see the sea by day from a gated veranda. The squares lend texture without blocking the view of sea and sky. Such picture imagining calls our attention to the power of value in creating shape, line, depth, and mood in compositions of simple elements. Over the unity of plaited patchwork, stitchery, and appliqué developing the theme can be most effective.

28

Blocks B and C are regular and soothing, traditional but with interesting things happening. Block D, less easily read, invites thought. Let's complicate matters further with the Type E Block Layout:

•Values of verticals neither symmetrical nor progressive, but mixed.

•Values of horizontals arranged symmetrically, but

•The number of strands in each vertical value set differ from the number of strands in each horizontal value set.

The pattern layout for block E in Plate 35 is Vrt: 5M, 5D, 5L. Hrz: 3M, 3D, 3L, 3D, 3M.

Notice first the large dark shapes that dominate this block. Find their negative image in light and their incomplete image in medium. Which value seems nearest? Which gets lost as background? Find long-stemmed crosses that borrow squares from their neighbors where value *contrast* is low. Checkerboards and solid areas are rectangular in this block where value groups of three cross value groups of five.

Rotate the block with the light area at top. Compare images in that position and with the light area at bottom. Compare the light-ray or pathway effect with that of block B turned on its side. This trick of filtering one light color through a checkerwork of changing values creates the illusion of a beam of light through a quilt.

The advantages of constructing a quilt from blocks multiply in lalanga quilts. For easy comparisons of blocks we have used the same number of strands the same width in our practice blocks. Photocopy these and try them in quilt layouts. Place the same block side by side for an overall layout. Alternate directions of the block. Mix block types. Sash them. Set them on point with solid alternate blocks. Wash copies with watercolor to preview the effect in cloth.

Future plaited blocks need not match in number and width of strands. They need not be square. Interesting quilts can be built from odd-size blocks and filler fabrics.

THE VALUE OF COLOR: MATS IN MINIATURE

Now that you appreciate value by itself and have some layout plans in your repertoire, let's add color. Let's plait in cloth strips with monochromatic color schemes like pale blue through navy or lavender through purple. Fusible transfer web on a cloth backing secures them. Work with rough edges or fray them slightly.

You need:

A pinboard that tolerates ironing. Styrofoam is not suitable.

Pins, scissors, ruler, rotary cutter and board desirable

Paper-backed fusible web (Trans-fuse™, Wonder-Under™, or similar)

Cloth strips cut ½" wide in three or more values of your chosen color. You may want a different color for each mat.

Cloth squares for backing, 9" squares for 15-strand mats, larger for larger mats.

Procedure:

1. Let's copy in cloth one of the 15-strand paper mats. Follow manufacturer's directions to fuse an 8" square of the web to the 9" square of backing fabric. Center it on the wrong side of the material. Peel off the paper. Why an 8" square?

You may have noticed that paper mats of 15 half-inch strands grew larger than 7½ inches. The thickness of horizontal strands passing between vertical strands forces expansion. This also happens with cloth, which you need to work slightly looser. The extra half inch is *expansion allowance.*

2. Pin the backing fabric to the center of the board, *fusible web side up.* Pin each corner.

3. Cut 9½" lengths of strips for the lights, mediums, and darks in your layout. Place verticals face up in the layout order, with the left edge of vertical one on the left edge of the *fusible web.* The bottom of each vertical is even with the bottom of the *backing fabric.* Each is pinned to the board just below the bottom edge of the fusible web. This layout places the actual weaving on the web, with ends protruding beyond.

Allow a *tiny* space between verticals. They need not reach the right-hand edge of the fusible web. Plate 37 (page 30) shows the complete vertical set-up for a type C block, with loose horizontals laid beside it for easy pick up.

4. Raise alternate verticals. Unlike paper, cloth does not crease. Just fold verticals lightly toward you. Lay in the first horizontal even with the fusing web. Pull its ends to straighten it; then let it relax. Pin both ends. As you see in

Plate 37.

Plate 38, raised verticals rest partly on the weaving board, easy to pick up for lowering.

5. Coordinate both hands to lower raised verticals and raise those already down. In raising, fold them loosely back to clear the way for the next horizontal. Do not pull them back, wrinkling the horizontal already in place. Experience will tell you how tightly to plait each type of strand. Continue adding horizontal rows, as you did in paper. Pin the ends of every horizontal (Plate 39).

6. Occasionally lower all verticals and look at the mat. If horizontals wrinkle, the tension of the verticals is too tight. Pat and massage the area to ease the verticals back. If the mat bulges at the center, or gaps appear in the weave, some strands are too loose. In Plate 40 I am pulling a loose strand to tighten the weave. My other hand steadies the surrounding strands. Leave pins in the edges of the mat until you have made any adjustments.

7. Remove most pins. Heat-fuse the mat right on the pinboard, according to manufacturer's directions for the web. Trim the strands. If desired, fold and stitch the backing to the front for a tidy frame. Alternately, trim just the backing. Frame the mat under glass, with strand ends showing. (Sign it, of course.) You can also machine stitch mats to sturdy paper for a notebook file. Plait several monochrome mats. Experiment with layout. Compare moods of the same layout in different hues. Add a fourth value to your layouts.

DOUBLE YOUR SCORE – IT'S REVERSIBLE

The fabric tubes in Chapter 2 make reversible

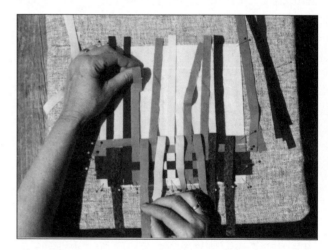

Plate 39.

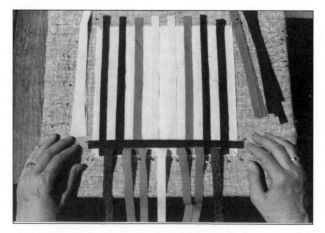

Plate 38.

Plate 40.

projects. Let's enlarge one of the sample blocks by increasing strand width. Change ½" strips into ¾" tubes, half again the width. This converts an 8" mat to a 12" mat.

Cut strips 2" wide (¾ + ¾ + ½ for seam allowance). This time you need not follow the monochrome rule strictly. If this mat suits a particular room, use that color scheme. Or spark a monochrome dark and medium with a flash of contrasting light.

A Formula for Tube Strand Length:

1. Vertical strands: Length = the *number* of horizontal strands x the *width* of horizontal strands, plus 10% *takeup* allowance, plus ½" for *edge finish.*

2. Horizontal strands: Length = the *number* of vertical strands x the *width* of vertical strands, plus 10% *takeup* allowance, plus ½" for *edge finish.*

Takeup varies with fabric thickness and need not be exact. Ten percent is safe for tube strands. Thus to convert block C in Plate 35 to ¾" tube strands you need: Vrt length = 15 Hrz x ¾" = 11¼"

10% of 11¼" = 1⅛"

edge finishing = ½"

Length of each vertical strand = 12⅞" (13")

Since you are using 15 verticals as well, the length of horizontals is the same – 13".

Count the total number of strands needed for each value. For example, block C takes 12D, 12M, and 6L.

Each strip before sewing measures 2" x 13". Since you can cut three of these from the full width of fabric, you need 8" of dark and medium and 4" of light. For efficient cutting and sewing, make tubes the full width of the fabric, minus selvedges. Turn the long tubes and cut them to the required length (four long dark tubes, four medium, and two light).

Procedure:

Lay out and pin vertical strands as for Plate 37, except that there is *no cloth backing.* Place pins about ¼" from the bottom ends of strands. Leave a *slight* gap between each strand.

Open the first row. Lay in and pin Hrz 1. Be sure that its ends extend at least ½" beyond the verticals at each side. The horizontal strand begins approximately ½" above the bottom ends

of verticals. Weave the row, leaving the second row open for Vrt. 2. Weave row 2 without opening row 3 yet. Look at the weave. No gaps should show at intersections, but neither should strands be wrinkled. Adjust the spacing of verticals if necessary.

Continue adding new rows, pinning horizontals at each end. At the top of the mat only *over-stroke* verticals need to be pinned. Ends of verticals should protrude ½" or so from the top, for finishing the mat.

Measure the lengths of sides and across the center of the mat in both directions. Adjust discrepancies by tightening or loosening the weave in appropriate places, and repin. Baste around all outside rows, securing ends of verticals near the outside edges of horizontals, and ends of horizontals near the outside edges of verticals. In Plate 41 you see that one stitch per strand is adequate.

Remove pins as you come to them. If you are right-handed start at the lower right-hand corner so that you have no pins to catch the thread loop as you draw it up. When finished, trim strand ends to about ¼" all around the mat.

Choose binding fabric, perhaps a shade from the mat or another that sets it off. Test by laying it beside the weaving and masking off all but ¼".

Cut four straight-grain binding strips 1½" longer than each side of the mat and 2" wide. Fold them lengthwise, right side out, and press. First bind the right and left sides of the mat. Pin the bindings to the reverse side of the mat, raw edges even with the trimmed ends of strands. Both ends of the binding extend ¾" beyond the top and bottom edges of the mat. Pin the bindings through

Plate 41.

most of the overstroke strands, just off the edge of the vertical strand and parallel to it (Plate 42).

Before sewing, check the reverse side to see that no vertical strand edges are caught by pins. Machine stitch just outside the edge of the vertical strand, even with the pins. Plate 43 shows how to stroke the edges of crossing strands with a long needle to prevent them from curling away from the presser foot. Use an even feed foot.

Fold the binding to the front of the mat and sew it by hand to cover the line of machine stitching. If the fit is tight, trim strand ends slightly to reduce seam allowance. *Do not cut off the ends of the bindings.*

Stitch the top and bottom bindings in the same manner, as in Plates 42 and 43. Their ends should extend at least ½" beyond the finished side bindings. Follow Figure 5 A–E to finish the corners. Do these before you sew the length of top and bottom bindings.

Plate 43.

Plate 42.

A. Begin and end stitching at the outside of the previously applied binding. *Then* trim that binding to less than ¼". The raw edges of the second binding extend beyond the trimmed end.

B. Turn the mat over to the back. Trim the second binding as shown. Cut the layer closest to you on a diagonal line passing just above the end of the stitching. Trim the seam allowance corner of the layer closest to the mat to a depth of ¼".

C. Turn the mat to the front. Fold the binding

out, ready to fold to the front. The trimmed angles now look like this.

D. Fold the end down to cover the finished binding.

E. Last, fold the second binding to the front of the mat. Secure the end with a pin. Hand stitch

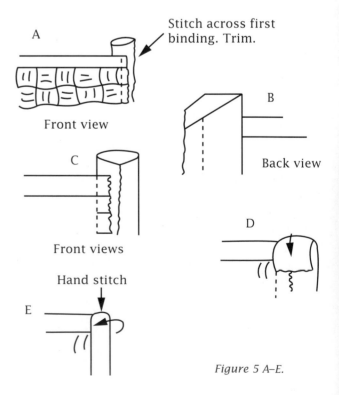

Figure 5 A–E.

from the outer corner across the end and the original binding. Tuck in escaping fabric with your needle. (See Figure 7 C.) Ladderstitch – alternating stitches through each side, then a pull to tighten – works well on such bulky joins.

Hand stitch the bindings on the front. Remove all basting and compare the two sides of the mat. Some pattern difference results from whether the first horizontal row begins over or under a vertical strand.

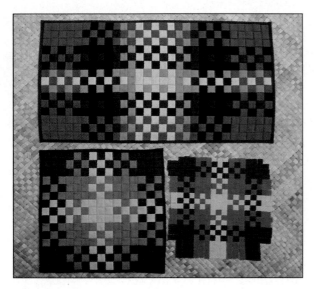

Plate 44.

Here is my brown C–type mat in tube plaiting, and the fabric practice version in muted pink/red (Plate 44). The long mat above them I designed by doubling block E. I substituted a fourth value for the light strands at the center, and used dark green and dark brown combined for the dark value. To keep an odd number of strands in the mat and in the center group, I removed one light vertical from the double layout. This kept the pattern in mirror image.

Here is my layout and the measurements for the long mat:

Vrt: 5M, 5D, 3L, 3 very L, 3L, 5D, 5M

13" long. Total Vrt equals D – 10, M – 10, L – 6, VL – 3

Hrz: 3M, 3D, 1L, 1VL, 1L, 3D, 3M.

25" long. Total Hrz equals D – 6, M – 6, L – 2, VL – 1.

I found it easier to keep the plait straight by turning the layout and using horizontals as verticals and vice versa. Do this when it suits your purpose.

A WORD ABOUT WASHING

I wash tube mats by hand, flat in a sink or bathtub. I let the wet mat drip, then stretch it on a thick towel pinned to the weaving board. I lay another thick towel over it and press down to let it absorb moisture. After the mat is almost dry in the pinned position, I press it. This is probably not necessary and they could go through the washing machine. I would not machine dry the mats, as this makes more wrinkles than it removes.

FLYING TIME

What happens if you fold three corners of your mats up to meet at the center, the way an envelope is folded? What if you ladderstitch the corners together and continue along the bindings as if gluing the seams of an envelope? What happens to the pattern? Look at the other side of the envelope as well. Which way do the colors run? What happens to the squares?

To use this as a bag, how could you fasten the flap? For a bag with a fabric lining and plaited outside, which of the techniques you now know might work? How else might you fold a mat to make a bag? How would the folding affect the fall of the pattern? How would you design a mat specifically for making into a bag?

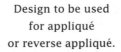

Design to be used
for appliqué
or reverse appliqué.

Chapter Four
BUT SERIOUSLY NOW:
A STRATEGY FOR LEARNING BY DOING

APPROACHING PLAITED DESIGN

Once you know a few things about a subject you can combine loose bits of information and ask, "What if?" In Chapter 1 we looked at the elements of lalanga designs and a few ways to vary them. Chapter 2 gave ways to construct fabric strands. In Chapter 3 you learned efficient hand movements while practicing:

Checkerwork weaving with same-width strands.

The horizontal/vertical setting of strands.

A planned layout of strands in light, medium, and dark values.

Organizing and writing layout patterns.

Fabric strand preparation and use with raw-edge strips and tube strands.

Plaitwork fused to a backing fabric.

Reversible plaitwork.

The bound-edge finish for mats.

Congratulations. You are now a beginner instead of someone who knows nothing about lalanga. Become an organized beginner, use what you already know as hooks on which to hang new information, and your ideas will multiply.

PERMUTATIONS

Most "new" ideas are recombinations of old elements. If you know how to cut and apply shapes to a backing and how to piece traditional quilt blocks, you can convert a Churn Dash

Plate 45.

block to "Cow in the Churn" (Plate 45). You've injected originality into your quilt, filled a bland area in the block's center, and shared a laugh. Permutation means combining known elements in new ways – the key idea of your learning strategy:

1. Permute skills you know as a basic plan for a project.

2. Ask for a new element. Make a problem for yourself.

3. Ask how to get around that problem.

4. Incorporate your solution into your stock of permutable elements. Remember – *A problem is not a reason why you can't.* It's a question, "What do I have to do, and is it worth it?"

Exercises: Let's make a series of cloth mat samples, asking, "What if?" Keep them for a reference notebook of permutations.

PROJECT ONE:

1. What if you use cloth strips ½" wide in horizontal/vertical checkerwork? What if you leave raw edges and prepare a fusible web backing big enough for 10 strands in each direction?

2. But what if you're bored with three values and symmetrical arrangements? You want more tints and shades and a sequence that doesn't repeat.

3. You could do what I did in these three samples:

Sample one: Use the same value for all vertical strands, as in the type A block, but cut 10 different values of the same hue for horizontals. Mix their order to see what happens. If you don't like the effect, try a different order. Fuse the one you like. My sample is in Plate 46.

Sample two: Again use the same value for all verticals. Shade horizontal values from bottom to top, as in the right-hand sample.

Sample three: Now use 10 light-to-dark values from left to right as verticals, and the same 10 values from bottom to top as horizontals. Do not look at color Plate 64 until you finish.

4. Add random and regular shading to your bag of tricks.

Plate 46.

PROJECT TWO:

1. What if you use three values of a color, *ironed-edge* strips, and horizontal checkerwork?

2. Make a real problem for yourself. Ask for a fancy mat edge instead of a bound one. Prairie points would be nice. What will you do with the ends of strands? How will you finish raw edges of the backing? How will you add the points?

3. You can borrow and adapt a Niue Island technique for turning points with the strands themselves. Look ahead at Plates 76 and 77, the elephant parade banner. Ends of rows are not ends of strands. Strands end *within* rows. Each row ends with an arrowhead turn that carries the strand into another row (above or below).

How are strand ends hidden? In firm, flat pandanus ends overlap and run together for several strokes. Each end hides under an overstroke on its own side of the mat. If you do that with cloth the overlap area will be thicker than the rest of the row.

This cloth mat is not reversible anyway. Your problem is keeping ends from pulling out from under the overstroke that hides them. You have already solved the problem with fusible web.

Other problems remain. If you use the Niuean turn, raw edges ironed to the backs of strands will show in the arrowhead. This is a special turn designed to equalize stress and keep the checker pattern. Instead, you can fold prairie points and trust the web to hold the row-end turns in place. You will also lay in rows differently. With narrow pandanus strands we climb continuously from row to row. With half-inch fabric strands, points would be obviously uneven. Values would change within rows instead of between them.

What do you do? Follow me through the pho-

tos for Project Two. Is it worth it? I couldn't have made the coat for "Sunset of the Weaver Wizards" without the Niuean turn and a lot of homework in pandanus and cloth.

Materials and Procedure for the Prairie Points Mat:

For a 12 x 12 row block you will use each strand of ironed-over edge strip for *two* of the rows. That is, one strip prepared equals two strands for weaving. Thus it must be twice the length needed for one row, plus enough for two prairie point turns, plus overlap and safety allowance. Remember that each row already contains takeup allowance.

Cut strips 1" wide. Fold and iron them to ½". Twelve of these side by side makes a mat width of 6" plus some expansion. Six inches plus *8 percent takeup allowance for ironed-over edge strands* (½") equals 6½". Two rows then require 13" before we add allowance for turning two points (2½") and 1" for overlap and safety. Each double strand needs 16½". The allowance for turning points is twice the width of the strand, plus ¼" ease at the turn. (2 x ½" + ¼" = 1¼" at each end of the row.) You will see how this works when you turn the points. They add one row width to each side of the mat.

Since each double strand makes two rows, you need six verticals and six horizontals each 16½" long. Make the six verticals light. Make four of the horizontals medium and two of them dark. We will use a horizontal layout of four rows medium, four dark, four medium.

For backing cut a 7½" square of fabric. Leave ¼" on all sides as you apply a 7" square of fusible web. This allows for 6½" covered with plaiting, plus ¼" of web on all sides for fusing a ¼" hem behind the prairie points. Turn the bottom and left-hand seam allowances over the web at this time and fuse-baste them. Leave the top and right-hand allowances until you find out exactly where your plaiting ends on those sides. Pin the backing to your board.

Follow Plate 47 (page 36) as you begin. Find the center point of one vertical (light) and one horizontal (medium) double strand. Place a pin 1" *below* the center of each, which gives you a longer segment and a shorter segment. Lay the longer segment of the vertical, right side up, parallel to the left edge of the backing and ¼" inside it. The pin you placed should be ¼" up from the

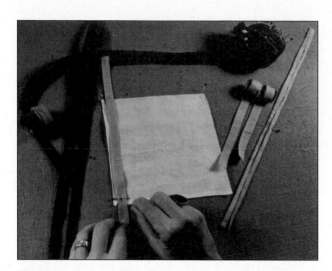

Plate 47.

Plate 49.

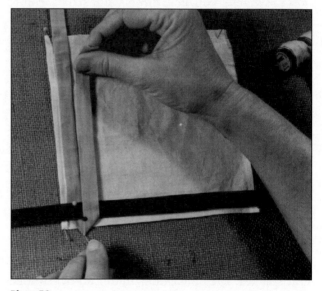

Plate 50.

bottom of the backing. Place a holding pin at this point, through strand, backing, and board.

As in Plate 48, lay the longer segment of the horizontal, right side up, parallel to the bottom edge of the board and ¼" inside it. The pin you placed through this strip should meet the outer edge of the vertical strip. Pin all layers to the board here and remove the other pins. You have established the commencement corner, commencement edge, and left-hand edge of the mat. Prairie points will extend beyond, partly covering the hem of the backing.

To turn the first prairie point (Plate 49) fold the short segment of the vertical strand under, at a 90° angle. Lay the strand parallel to the horizontal strand. A pin helps to turn and crease the

Plate 48.

strand at a 45° angle to the strands themselves. Pin the point of the prairie point.

To complete the turn, fold the vertical strand upward, across the horizontal strand and parallel to vertical strand 1 (Plate 50). This conceals all raw edges, makes the first checker stroke, and establishes vertical strand 2.

Before turning a prairie point with the horizontal strand, open the new horizontal row by raising vertical strand 1. Then fold the short segment of the horizontal strand under, exposing the raw edges and bringing it parallel to the left-hand edge. Pin the point (Plate 51).

As in Plate 52, fold the horizontal strand up, completing the prairie point. It lies above horizontal 1 and becomes horizontal 2.

Lower vertical 1 (by my left hand in Plate

Plate 51.

53). You now have two prairie points forming the commencement corner, and the beginnings of two vertical and two horizontal rows. Raise horizontal 1 (in my right hand) to open a row for the next vertical strand.

In placing vertical 3, judge length by eye. This time use the *short* segment, so that even-numbered strands will be long. This makes the last long strand fall at the outer edge of the mat. You do not want overlap in outside rows. Turn a prairie point with the long segment of vertical 3 and weave in vertical 4. Plate 54 shows verticals 3 and 4 established and vertical 5 going in.

Continue adding vertical pairs until you have laid in vertical 11 and begun to turn the prairie point for placing vertical 12. Plate 55 shows that horizontal 2 has run out at this point.

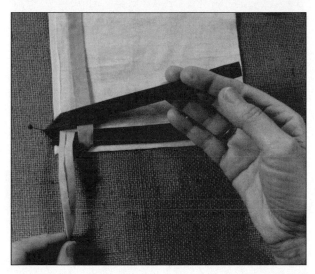

Plate 52.

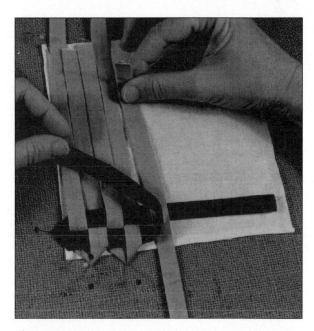

Plate 54.

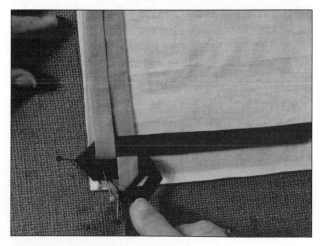

Plate 53.

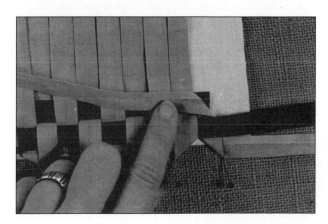

Plate 55.

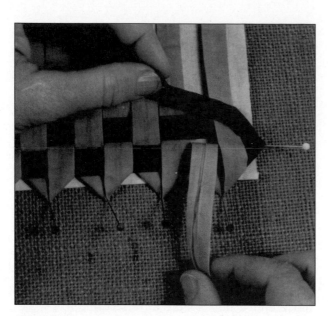

Plate 56.

Weave your mat up to this stage. When you lay in Hrz 11, use the *short* segment, ending under Vrt 10. Notice that alternating Vrts have run out. You must trim them under Hrz 11. Pin Hrz 11 to the board through its lower edge, so that pins secure every vertical to be trimmed. Pin Vrt 2 through Hrz 10, which is its last understroke before the edge row.

Plate 57.

Trim it back to occupy about half the space under vertical 11, on the web.

Complete the prairie point and lay in vertical 12. Leave vertical 11 raised. As in Plate 56, turn a prairie point at the right-hand edge, using horizontal 1. Bring the tail of horizontal 1 into the open row to overlap horizontal 2. Lower vertical 11 and place a pin through all layers, into the board. Leave the protruding tail until the completed mat has been fused. You have completed the first two horizontal rows and set up all verticals.

Open the next horizontal row by lifting vertical strands in checker. Lay in another medium value horizontal strand. Begin with the long segment of every horizontal pair, so that the overlap join falls in the second row you weave. This overlap may fall under any vertical except an outside one. Staggering the overlaps makes the mat more even, so lay in new horizontals so their ends will fall at different places. Look at Plate 57, in which ten horizontal rows have been completed.

Abbreviations. At this point let's start to use those convenient abbreviations for horizontals and verticals, as knitters read a knitting pattern. If you can locate the overlap pins in Hrz 2, 4, 6, and 8, you will see what I mean about staggering overlaps by laying in Hrzs at different sections of their length. Note also that I changed values for rows 5 through 8 and returned to the original value in row 9.

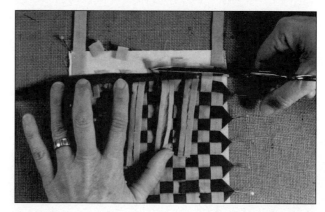

Plate 58.

Roll Hrz 11 back and trim Vrt 3, 5, 7, 9, and 11(Plate 58). Return Hrz 11 to its normal position and lower all raised Vrts to complete row 11 as much as possible. The Vrts you would raise for row 12 have been cut off.

Vrt 2 is trimmed under Hrz 10. In Plate 59 you see the pin and the missing overstroke in row 11. Vrt 1 is raised to admit Hrz 12 to the last row.

Plate 59.

Plate 61.

With Vrt 1 turn a prairie point to the right. Lead its end under Hrz 12. With tweezers, draw it under Hrz 10 to overlap the end of Vrt 2 (Plate 60). Repin the overlap.

Continue turning the long ends of remaining Vrts as prairie points to finish vertical rows. You will turn them from right to left in all remaining rows. Stop when you have only one Vrt left to turn.

laps Vrt 11 under Hrz 11. Pin it, as Hrz 11 is pinned through Vrt 10 next to it.

Plate 62.

Plate 60.

Finish Hrz row 12 and turn that prairie point before you finish Vrt row 12. Plate 61 shows tweezers leading the end of Hrz 12 (now Hrz 11) under Vrt 12. Continue over the cut end of Vrt 11 and under Vrt 10. Pin the overlap.

Use Vrt 12 to turn the last prairie point, at the end of the top row. In Plate 62 its tail over-

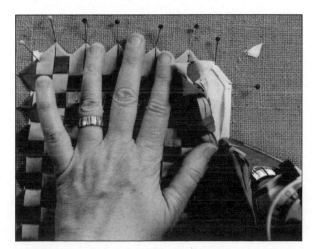

Plate 63.

Working with one edge at a time, remove just the pins through the prairie points. If the backing shows beyond the points trim it even with them. Trim all corners diagonally, in a line even with the edges of corner prairie points. Fold the raw edges in and fuse-baste. Fold raw edges of the sides just under the edge of the actual weaving, in a similar position to the edges you hemmed before beginning the mat. Fuse-baste the outside row of the weaving.

Continue around all sides of the mat, removing pins as you go. Finally, remove overlap pins and permanently fuse the whole mat. When it cools trim the protruding ends of overlaps to hide them.

While fusing web should hold under normal use, you could add decorative machine stitching inside the points, perhaps with meanders across the grid.

More Value in Color

Plate 64 Top row: The left-hand mat plays black verticals over a random array of brown values in the horizontals. In the center mat, brown values shade upward from light to dark. The ten reds and pinks of the right-hand mat shade from dark to light in both horizontals and verticals. Bottom row: Prairie point mats secured by fusible web backing employ the type A layout turned in different directions. In the ribbon mat at left, light peach and green contrast in hue but not much in value. The center mat is the one we just finished, and the right-hand mat a higher-contrast version.

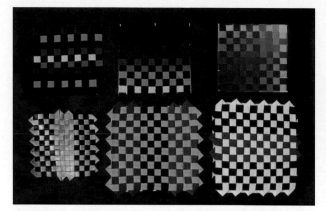

Plate 64.

FLYING TIME – WHAT IF?

What if you turn color Plate 64 on point and look at each prairie point mat separately? What happens at the corners? If you wanted to use the ribbon mat on a garment or accessory, where would you place it? What sort of surrounding fabric would you choose? How would you secure it in place?

What if you fold these mats envelope style, as in our last flying time? What problems arise? What do you have to do? Does any worthwhile result ensue?

Do you remember the Greek legend of the army that arose from a field after the hero sowed dragon's teeth? The soldiers fought, and only the strongest five survived to join forces and become the ancestors of a great city. Ideas are like that, so sow dragon's teeth, and may the best ideas win.

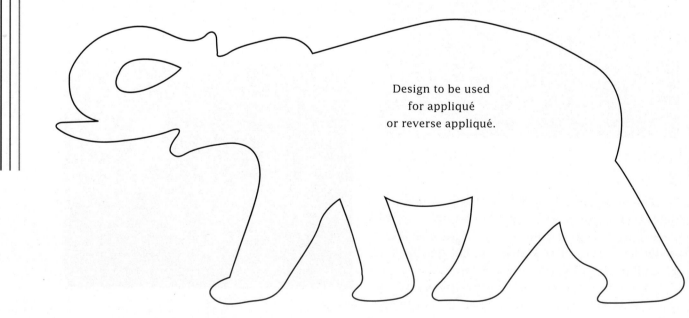

Design to be used
for appliqué
or reverse appliqué.

Chapter 5

Pattern Within Pattern:
The Advantage of Cloth

Every technique you add to your repertoire adds complexity – new factors to juggle, more decisions to make. You have learned how value contrast creates the patterns of lalanga. The same is true of patterns in print fabric. Designers juggle contrasts of value, hue, and intensity.

In plaited patchwork you lay out an overall pattern, then complicate the units of that pattern – the squares – with patterns of printed fabric. Does that sound like what you've been doing all along with conventional quilt designs?

The mats and blocks you have made thus far employ narrow strands. Like quilts with many small pieces, their values and solid hues are visually complex enough to be interesting. If we use prints with wider strands we maintain that level of complexity. On the other hand, we can escalate the game with prints *and* narrow strands.

Let's survey some considerations in using prints, then study examples.

1. Each piece you make has an *overall contrast effect* employing value, hue, and intensity. For drama you can use maximum contrast, the pattern sharply defined. At the other extreme, low contrast creates a rich, subtle surface. Or the degree of contrast can vary within the piece, subtle in some areas, dramatic in others. This effect may appear carefully planned or the result of happy accident.

2. Plaiting is useful for exploring color. Your pattern layout controls the fall of hues, values, and intensities and sets the proportion of each of these in the piece. It's hue that engages your emotions. You often use it intuitively, but the standard art formulas can help you get started.

Monochromes (same-hue schemes) give minimum contrast. Complementaries (opposites on the color wheel) give maximum contrast. Analogous schemes (close neighbors on the wheel) can trick the eye into seeing more hues than are actually present.

Add to these color *intensity*. A highly saturated red glows among grayed companions, as yellow raincoats appear brilliant in the rain.

3. Print characteristics affect their role in patchwork. Some have a high-contrast pattern that remains distinct at a distance. Others read as textured solids, even up close. Scales of prints vary from huge to tiny, their figures from close together to widely scattered. The mood of their subject matter influences the mood of your project.

4. Finally, the layout of your composition – shaded, balanced, or organized in some other fashion – can become more complex through adding prints.

OVERALL CONTRAST

As a quilter you recognize the patchworks that call to you across a crowded room. Others say little at a distance but hold your interest face to face while you search for their identities among lovely complexities. Then there are the charmers that reveal *and* conceal. You walk across the room to meet them, often back and forth across the room several times. What is this magic language? It's contrast – value assisted by hue and intensity.

Strong contrast over the entire surface claims immediate attention. You see the pattern at once.

Plate 65.

What happens then depends on the arrangement and complexity of the shapes. Overall high contrast need not be boring (Plate 65).

Low contrast extinguishes the pattern. Color and texture come to the fore. In searching out shapes and the boundaries between them, the eye notes details, small clues it would miss if hypnotized by the force of strong contrast.

Plate 66. Badges of fringed strip secured with fusing web and metallic machine and hand stitching feature the New Zealand kiwi bird and a rose. The foundation cloth is laced over padded plastic.

The green nature badge in Plate 66 and the plaited squares on the blouse in Plate 67 use low contrast to shift attention to the colored metallic stitching, the soft frayed edges of strands, and the indefinite prints. The nature badge details include french knots and braided loose threads trailing from the ends of its strands. On the purple blouse, flyaway strand ends and painted squiggles and dots soften the transition between plaited squares and plain background. They unify the composition by repeating elements of the plaitwork in a different way.

In the rose garden badge (Plate 66), contrast shades from almost none at the upper right to moderate at lower left. This comes from shading both horizontal and vertical values, with solid color verticals darkening faster. This piece lies on the borderline of patchwork employing a mix of high and low contrast.

The yellow and black block in Plate 68 and the triangular autumn hanging in Plate 69 show contrast shaded from low to moderately high. This is *not* the same as shading values of *strands*. In Plate 68 the block's strands shade

Plate 67. Rayon batik scraps from a garment factory make easily frayed plaiting strips. Fusible web and machine meanders hold them.

Plate 68. A shading exercise with prints and solids chosen only for their values. Half-inch strands.

from dark at the bottom and left, to light at the top and right. Contrast is low at the lower left, upper right, and center because *strands of similar values cross there.* High contrast appears at the upper left and lower right, where light and dark strands cross.

Plate 69. For an autumn hanging, half a square is plaited and turned on point. Strands approximately a half inch wide.

In the autumn hanging, low contrast occurs where medium value strands cross at left and center. Contrast is stronger at the right where lighter strands cross darker. This changing contrast represents the passage of time. Autumn evolves from the rich confusion of russet leaves into the starkness of bare tree forms against pale stubble fields awaiting the snow.

We mix high and low contrast in symmetrical layouts of light, medium, and dark strands. Look back at block C in Plate 35. The central light area attracts your attention first. Then you notice the strong checkers at each edge of the block, and last the weak checkers on either side of them.

Repeating any of blocks A through E regularly over a quilt surface gives a predictable mixed contrast effect. Repeating them in unpredictable order and position, or changing the values within each repeating block could give you a charmer. Print strands raise your unpredictability quotient.

This overall distribution of contrast may be the last thing you learn to control. It's easy to plan value contrast in a layout. Adding hue, intensity, and the characteristics of print means juggling many variables. You are in for surprises. Enjoy them.

HUE AND INTENSITY

The nature badge and autumn hanging use greens and browns as monochromatic schemes. Additionally, those hues are toned down from the pure colors. (Brown is derived from orange and its closest neighbors.) The rust in the autumn piece is the least toned and therefore appears bright compared to its neighbors.

The block in Plate 68 spreads sideways from monochrome. Its yellows wander off into brown territory and quite legitimately consort with the neutrals black and cream. High intensity yellow contrasts with low intensity browns and dirty yellows.

The rose garden introduces the complementary color scheme. Did you expect complementaries to shout? Magenta and green lie opposite on the color wheel, but Rose Garden uses low-intensity greens and pink tints. Pink warms the compostion rather than setting up a dialogue.

For intense complementary conversation, look at the meetings of green and pink in the summer wallhanging, Plate 70, and of purple and yellow in Plate 71.

These pieces use complementary-plus-analogous schemes. One of the complementary colors expands sideways to pick up its neighbors. In the summer hanging, all verticals are green, but played against them are horizontals of yellow, orange, fuchsia, magenta, and violet.

Plate 70. In the summer hanging intense color and frayed unruly edges represent the rampant growth of burgeoning summer.

43

Plate 71.

In Plate 71 the hand-dyed tube strands of the skirt of "Sunset of the Weaver Wizards" employ two *sets* of analogous colors which cross in the weave. Sometimes the complements yellow and violet cross in the weave, producing a strongly contrasting checker pattern. Sometimes the analogous yellow, orange, red-orange, red, and magenta cross, producing a glow. Likewise

associations of red, red-violet, and purple inspire the eye to mix an intense violet. (See the whole costume in Plate 130 for the overall contrast effect.)

Low-intensity analogous color creates delicate washes. Prints in Plate 67 cover half the color wheel, from blue-violet to almost-yellow. Because most are grayed, a few flashes of orange, gold, and purple look more intense than they really are. These plaited squares virtually designed themselves, as one print nominated the next. The blouse must be a charmer. People cross crowded rooms to ask about it.

STUDYING PRINTS AND
PATTERN CHARACTERISTICS

View Plate 72 up close and at a distance. Every other print contains strong *contrasts* of value, hue, or intensity. The prints in between contain little contrast. Which prints appear as solids as you move away from them? They can work as solids in your overall composition and still provide close-up complexity.

Which prints appear as broken shapes at a distance? They add interest to an overall composition. In "Weaverthink," Plate 163, one 'contrasty' large-scale print sprinkles confetti over an otherwise disciplined composition.

The *scale* of a print affects distance and

Plate 72.

44

appearance and what you get by cutting it into small squares. Large-scale prints reveal different hues and values as they play peek-a-boo through a plaited row. While this unpredictability adds surprise, their built-in harmony helps blend the overall composition. The "Weaverthink" print contains all the hues and values of the other prints and solids, except the lightest yellow. It adds a flash of white not present elsewhere. Note the large-scale prints in Plates 67, 68, and 69.

Small-scale prints give textural interest to large squares, or make subject matter and the full color range visible in small squares. Small prints in Plate 66 show leaves and flowers to suit the nature themes.

Along with scale consider pattern *density* and the way in which its elements are arranged. Flowers or geometrics scattered widely may not even appear in some squares. Motifs may run in rows on grain, so that the same object repeats the length of the plaiting strand. You may or may not want this. Dots, stripes, and plaids can be effective.

Moods of prints are often the most useful characteristic for your purpose. Most of us design on an emotional level. We want to create a feeling or express a theme. Our color and pattern choices follow.

Fabric mood is an elusive combination of subject matter and color. Designers of fabrics understand how color and scale affect our emotions and perceptions. They know that we associate blue and green with nature and tranquility. They know that we perceive large bright objects as near and small misty objects as far away. They have studied the motifs and art conventions of many cultures. We can select a designed fabric for its mood or theme, then build our other choices around it.

In the array in Plate 72 the large-scale blue and gold leaf and seashell fabric suggests tropical islands. Any print three places on either side of it could fit a composition about sun-washed exotic lands.

In contrast, the scrolled monochrome green print and its two green companions could leap over the jazzy neon jukebox fabric, all the way to the old-fashioned pink floral. Put a Vivaldi tape on the stereo, and you're weaving in an eighteenth century garden.

The bag in Plate 73 combines a dark, low intensity array of mysterious gold-brushed

Plate 73. Inside the magic bag, dark hints of color cover pockets concealing mysterious surprises. Low contrast and low intensity accentuate small flashes of more intense color.

prints with a background of magician's stars. These fabrics would make an effective woven panel for a matching garment.

Sometimes the idea, or the colors of reality, set a more difficult lalanga exercise. For the theme quilt "Plait Time in the Melting Pot – Aotearoa Stew Retains Its Flavours" (Plate 78) I selected prints to represent various ethnic groups living in New Zealand. Ideology overrode color theory. Green represented the land, with red and black for the founding Maori culture. Nothing but brown would do for Pacific Islands traditional bark cloth. The mood of celebration called for intense color as well. Eliminating blues and purples, I let intuition take over from there. Value and layout pulled the diverse strands together, with help from the artist's great friend black.

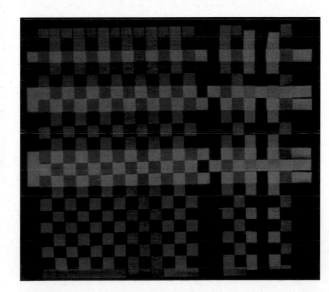

Plate 74.

45

PLANNING LAYOUT

You have worked with balanced, shaded, and random layouts, discovering some natural laws of checkerwork plaiting. You know that symmetrical balance requires an odd number of strands, but patterns need not be symmetrical. Plate 64 shows this and reminds you that the prairie point turn works for an even number of strands only. What else should you remember when planning layouts with prints? How does the number of strands of each fabric affect overall appearance? Plate 74 gives a sampler of these effects, in values only for simplification.

•A *single* strand of a particular hue, value, or print appears as a row of squares. The higher the contrast with the strands it crosses, the more pronounced the effect.

If crossing strands differ in hue, value, or intensity they may alter the *apparent* hue, value, and intensity of the single strand. You may hardly believe that it *is* the same strand. Strongly contrasting single strands lead the eye in the direction of their movement. By making gradual changes in single strands we can wash color across the surface.

•Two similar strands appear as a zigzag of squares.

Two horizontals crossing two verticals makes the familiar Four-Patch, two crossing three, a pyramid.

•Three similar strands form a balanced band of squares in which crosses may change places as the eye changes its perceptions.

Three crossing three makes a Nine-Patch cross.

•Larger sets of similar strands form checkerboards.

Medium- and low-contrast checkerboards function as *areas*, like large pieces of fabric in the overall composition of a quilt.

STRATEGIES FOR USING PRINTS IN PLAITING

The obvious, safe way of selecting prints is to choose a strong one you like very much. Accompany it with solids, textures, and less dominant prints that repeat its hues and values. Do estimate the *proportions* of the hues in that print. Consider this in deciding how much of the supporting fabric to use in your layout.

For example, the pink and black floral in Plate 72 has mostly pinks, with black ground color and accents of deep red and greens. You

can preserve the light but dramatic feeling, which may be why you like that fabric. Use more pink than black in your overall composition, then include small accents of deep red and green. These might not be whole strands, but just touches of color contained in a supporting print.

For more drama, you could call that floral "pink" and use it as the accent feature of a black mat shot with murky deep reds and greens. Or you could weave a mat about tints and shades of pink and toned red, incorporating the print for its peek-a-boo surprises.

To increase the interest of a scheme based on a dominant print, take a risk. Combine the print with fabrics that extend its scheme. These can be darker, lighter, or have more contrast. They can spread hues sideways on the color wheel, or add a flash of the complement for accent. The cushion cover in Plate 75 takes green from the dominant print for some additional strands. But the "red" print that sparks it contains deep yellow and magenta not in the original print. These, the grayed lavender, and the rust are analogous extensions of reds and pinks in the dominant print. Notice how using the original print for the border "floats" contrasting squares and softens the edges of the plaited area.

Plate 75.

You can also use fairly low contrast small prints for their hue and value only. The badges, blouse, yellow block, and autumn hanging are examples. Here many prints can blend one row into another, like a watercolor wash.

PRACTICE BLOCKS

With one inch or wider fabric strips, plait temporary compositions. Save those you like for reference and recycle the rejects.

•Plait a horizontal wash through solid color verticals, perhaps black. If black feels too harsh, try dark brown, green, navy, or purple. Lay in print horizontals shifting gradually in hue – perhaps from blue-green, to green, to yellow-green, on to sunshine yellow. Use about a dozen verticals long enough to cross 20 horizontals and see how many hue gradations you can select. Repeat the exercise with white or cream verticals.

•Now try verticals of one print, with a wash of solids and texture prints.

•Next shade both horizontals and verticals as I did for the badges. Try this with hue and also with value.

•Finally, plait some balanced layouts including prints.

APPLYING YOUR KNOWLEDGE

Why not experiment on garments? Iron fusible web onto garment areas to be covered. Insert a heat-proof weaving board into the garment. Plait the decoration and fuse it in place. Fringe or trim strand ends, then machine over the plaiting to embellish and hold it securely.

Pin the paper-backed pieces of fusible web in place while wearing the garment in front of a mirror. I shifted those paper squares on the purple blouse many times to develop a diagonal placement flattering to both front and side views. With raw-edge plaiting, hand-wash the garment.

PERMUTATION TIME

Have you had enough warm-up exercises? Set yourself a problem. Let's apply color and prints to a reversible banner made from tube strands. I'll tell you how I made mine, and you can decide how to make yours. Read through the method, then look ahead to see what I made. By then you will have ideas of your own.

You can use any width strand, any even number of verticals and horizontals, and any finished size, from window accent to room divider. I said "even number" because prairie points make a great edging for a hanging mat. Thus we need a Niuean set-up with pairs of verticals and horizontals. The formula for calculating lengths of these double strands is similar to that for the

fused mats in Chapter 4. Because we're using tube strands, use 10% takeup allowance.

LENGTH OF VRT:

Multiply number of Hrz x width of Hrz.

Add the width of two more rows for prairie points.

Add 10% takeup allowance, which includes takeup on points.

Double the result, for two strands from one tube.

Add overlap allowance the width of one strand or so.

LENGTH OF HRZ:

Multiply number of Vrt x width of Vrt.

Add the width of two more rows for prairie points.

Add 10% takeup allowance, including for points.

Double the result.

Add overlap allowance.

By deciding to use the double-strand set-up I made another choice. Fabrics change every two, four, or six rows. This makes choices of fabric simpler. That's just as well. This banner is reversible, so why not take advantage of that? What if our fabric tubes have different sides? We can use two basic plans for that. Take your pick.

A. Choose a dominant print plus companion prints and textures for one side of the banner. Back each print with the solid that best blends with it. Choose different solids to go with different prints. This gives a complex mix of pattern on one side of the banner and a strong pattern of squares on the other. I started my fabric choice this way. You will notice some modification.

B. Choose a dominant print, perhaps large scale. Back it with its major solid color. On the same side of the banner as the dominant print use harmonizing solids. Back each solid with a print. One side of the banner will have drama, the other a quieter interest.

MAKING DOUBLE-FACE TUBE STRANDS

Sew the strips of print and solid together, wrong side out, along one edge only. Press this seam to one side. Fold the tube right side out and press the folded edge. This makes it easier to press the other seam when the time comes. At this point you can plait with these half-finished strips to preview the project. If you want to change a fabric you have only one seam to unpick. Remember that these preview strands are wider than they will be after you sew the second seam. Expect to run out of *length* when previewing. To finish the strands, fold them wrong side out. Stitch the second edge seam. Turn the tube and press this second seam, assisted by having already pressed the first seam. The pin-and-pull system works well. Store pressed strands on a hanger or lay them flat.

A Different Point

Let's ask for one more change. Study the points of the fused mats in Plate 64. What if we want squares and triangles instead of the crochet-hook appearance of prairie points? The original Niuean arrowhead turn was designed to keep plaiting strokes in checker, with triangles at the point. These will connect the two sides of a banner by showing one triangle of the reverse

fabric at each turn. Figure 6 shows the Niuean arrowhead turn.

A. Place Vrt 1.

B. Fold Vrt 1 upward and to the right, revealing the reverse side.

C. Fold Vrt 1 upward and away from you. The original side comes to the surface as Vrt 2.

D. Lift Vrt 1 to open the row. Note the triangle at bottom.

E. Lay in Hrz 1. Lower Vrt 1. This gives checker squares over checker triangles.

F. Fold Hrz 1 under and away from you. The checker triangle at left shows its reverse side.

G. Fold Hrz 1 under and to the right. Its original side comes to the surface as Hrz 2. Lift Vrt 2 to open the row for it.

H. The start is complete. Continue adding Vrt until the layout is complete. Then work the Hrz rows as for mats in Chapter 4. *At the right-hand edge of the mat fold Hrz upward first, then under. Always fold these points in whatever direction makes the triangle.* Note: for a banner, which will not have points at the top, you can start arrowhead turns at the centers of vertical strands.

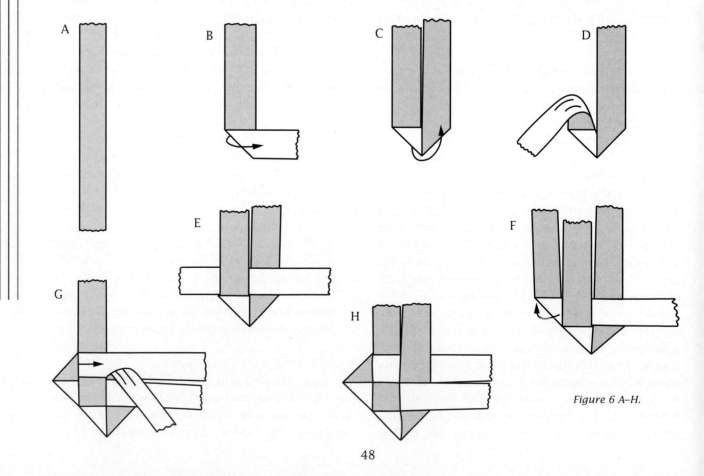

Figure 6 A–H.

48

JOINING TUBE STRANDS

The ends of horizontal row 2 must be joined by hand in the second row before you add row 3. Lower all verticals and check their spacing. Make adjustments if needed, *before* you sew the ends of horizontals.

The seams are less visible on prints than on solids, so I make joins where the print side of the strand is an overstroke and the solid side lies on top of a crossing strand that hides it on the other side of the mat. Figure 7 shows the steps.

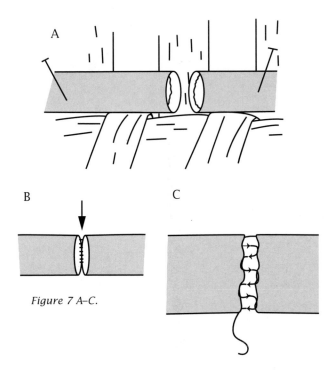

Figure 7 A–C.

A. Trim ends so that they overlap slightly less than 1". Turn raw ends of both ends inside and finger press the crease. The pins hold strands to the board so that you have the meeting place exactly right when creasing the seam.

B. Begin to ladderstitch the edges of the bottom side of the strand. Remove the pins so that you can get your fingers underneath after the first stitch or two. It's too difficult to stitch without lifting the strand. Complete the side of the strand away from you.

C. Continue stitching the side closest to you. Ladderstitch does not show on the surface. Loosely stitch through edge folds, then pull to tighten every few stitches.

When working with long strands, machine stitch strips of fabric together before making the strands. Press these seams open to reduce bulk.

Stagger the joins of plain and print fabrics. Try to make these joins fall so that they are hidden on the solid side.

ANOTHER TECHNICAL PROBLEM

Pandanus is firm; fabric sags. Hanging a fabric mat makes cross strands ooze downward, causing gaps above and wrinkles below. *Before you read on* quickly jot down as many ways as you can think of to prevent this.

Here are some of my thoughts:
- Hand-tack many strand intersections invisibly.
- Baste the mat, then machine quilt with invisible nylon thread on the solid side and thread that blends with the prints in the bobbin.
- Baste, then free-machine quilt wandering lines with colored threads that appear and disappear as they cross different fabrics.

But I didn't do any of those. I turned a problem into a plus with a South Pacific decorative device that stabilizes as well – the tied tassel. With colored pearl cotton and metallic threads and cord, the tassels enliven the plain side of the banner.

I left it pinned to the board, adding more pins through the main body of the weave. I basted the sides just inside the arrowheads. Tassels down the right and left sides of the mat and across the bottom hold verticals and horizontals together between the arrowheads. Tassels and charms hold some intersections in every row of the mat. Both decoration and function told me where to tie. For convenience in stitching I removed pins immediately in the way, then replaced them to prevent shifting before the tying was completed. Work with the board on a table.

For tassels with no stitches visible on the reverse of the mat:

A. Use 2 or 3 strands #8 pearl cotton or similar, 20" long, doubled in a crewel needle (large eye, sharp point). At the strand intersection stitch through the top layer only of each tube strand. The dotted line represents the thread *hidden* between layers, *not* individual stitches. The needle emerges through the folds of tube strands. The number of threads you see in the drawing is reduced for clarity.

Note that beginning and ending stitches overlap, leaving tails at both ends. If you have trouble pulling the needle through, use needlenose pliers to pull.

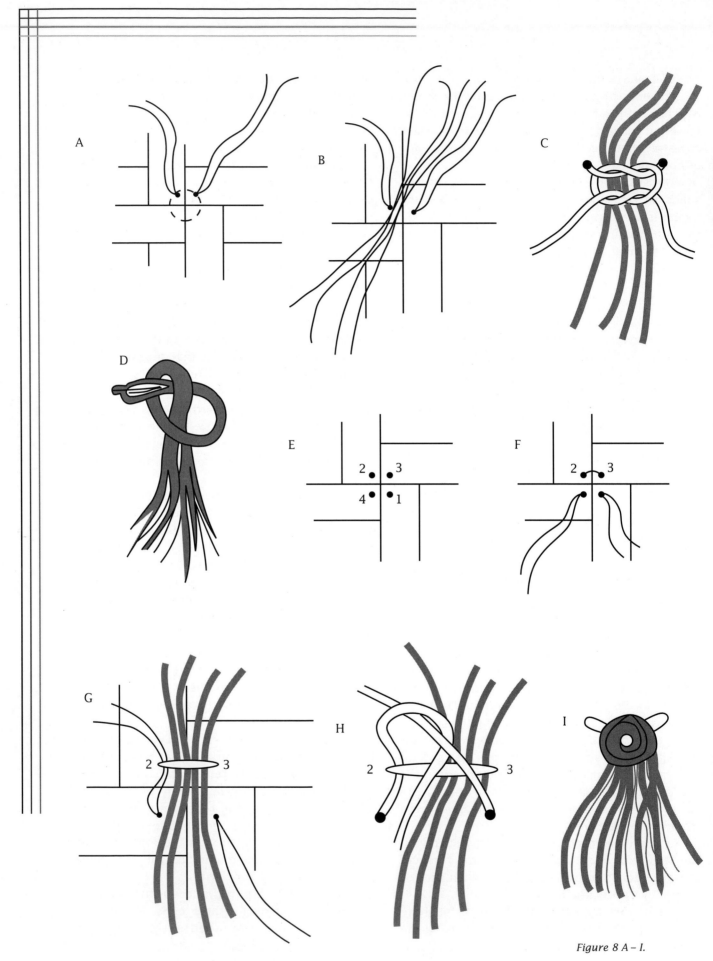

Figure 8 A – I.

B. Lay in 4 to 6 new threads about 10" long. Mix colors and thread types to complement the fabric at that intersection.

C. Tie the original ends in a square knot over the new threads.

D. Twist all threads together and tie an overhand knot. Push the knot against the fabric. A latch hook helps to tie overhand knots. Trim the tassel or leave ends uneven.

Sometimes I want a tassel on one side of a mat, and a large cross stitch visible on the other side:

E. With 22" strands of pearl cotton doubled in the needle, stitch straight down and straight up through all mat strands – down at 1, up at 2, down at 3, up at 4. Check your X on the back.

F. The front looks like this.

G. Take the nearest tail, plus 4 to 6 new threads, under the bar. Use a latch or crochet hook.

H. Knot the *original* ends across the bar and the new threads.

I. Knot all threads overhand and push the knot up.

HANGING THE BANNER

One problem remains. If this banner is reversible, how will we hang it? A sleeve on the back spoils the pattern on that side. Again, jot down the solutions you think of.

I bound the top edge of mine and added a rod pocket at the same time. It could have been a quiet, invisible little rod pocket in the least noticeable fabric of the banner. But I decided to make it a feature, continuing the theme of the banner. Here's how.

A. Measure the width of the mat, *not* includ-ing the points. Add 3" for doubled hems. Measure the circumference (distance around) the rod and add at least 3". Add more if you want a deep decorative heading like mine, 2" for every extra inch of depth. Cut the rod pocket fabric to those measurements.

Cut a firm lining fabric in a similar color, 3" shorter than the pocket (equal to the width of the woven mat). Lay it on the rod pocket fabric, wrong sides together, centered. Baste or fuse the lining in place.

Fold the ends of the rod pocket in ¼" and press. Fold them in again, over the ends of the lining, to hem the rod pocket to a width ⅛" longer than the width of the weaving. This is allowance for the pocket to extend a *fraction* beyond the weaving, instead of the other way around. Stitch by hand or machine.

B. Fold the rod pocket right side out, as for a regular binding. Trim the ends of vertical strands ⅜" outside the edge of the top horizontal strand. (You have basted the top as for any mat.) Pin the rod pocket to the "backs" of verticals, so that it protrudes slightly at either end of the weaving. Machine stitch. Trim verticals and seam allowance to ¼". See the side view, Step B.

C. Flip the rod pocket up. Press the seam. Mark a line on its *inside* layer that will reach the stitching line when you fold the binding (rod pocket) over the front of the mat. The line is about ⅞" above the seam. Crease the inside layer along this line.

D. Match and pin this crease to the machine stitching, including the lining of the inside layer. By hand, sew this binding to the mat front. The remaining fabric forms the rod pocket. See the

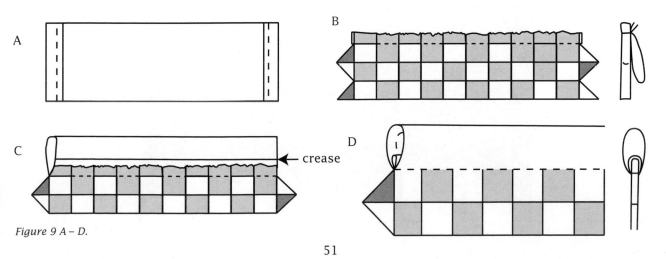

Figure 9 A – D.

51

side view, raw edges and strand ends covered by this inner binding. Ladderstitch ends of the inner binding closed.

An option: For a hanging with an odd number of verticals and no points at the bottom, such a rod pocket binding at both ends is attractive. What might you use for interesting rods?

WHEN ELEPHANTS LAST
IN THE MAIN STREET LOOMED

An Indian sari print from Fiji and a brown woodgrain print that looks like elephant hide brought back memories of circus parades and watching menagerie animals unloaded in the night. Elephants swayed under the stars in bejewelled costumes, bells tinkling, tassels swinging. This banner is a memorial for elephants, circuses, and childhood (Plates 76 and 77).

TECHNICAL NOTES FOR YOUR USE AS DESIRED

Finished size 27" wide x 38" long, including heading.

Plate 76.

Measurements: 6 double Vrt two-sided tube strands. Each fabric strip cut 2½" x 72". 8 double Hrz two-sided tube strands. Each fabric strip cut 2½" x 60". Rod pocket strip cut 10½" wide for parade space.

Tassels and embellishments: 3 strands #8 pearl cotton doubled for stitching, variegated and solids; 4 strands #8, #5, Kreinik #16 and #32 metallic braid, shiny rayon threads for laying in; buttons, bells, sequins, gilded seashells, soapstone charms, old jewelry, scented sandalwood beads. Synthetic gold leather elephants glued and stitched by machine with smoke-tone invisible thread and a #80 needle. Extra heavy tassels improve the hang of bottom corners.

Pockets: These hold charms, small dolls, messages, etc. They also stabilize strand crossings. Ladderstitch pocket bottoms on the side of the banner that will have the pocket, the overstroke side. Ladderstitch pocket *sides* on the reverse side of the banner, where objects would otherwise fall out. Catch only one layer of fabric from the understroke, so that the stitches do not show on the reverse side of the banner.

Blending in a too-strong element: On the print side of the banner, the blue triangles in the arrowhead turns seemed too strong. I reduced their impact by painting gold stars on them to connect them with the blue and gold star fabric. Were you wondering what happened to the plain blue strands from the reverse side?

FLYING TIME – CAN ANALYSIS BE HELPFUL?

Analyze the autumn hanging in Plate 69. Hold the book with the upper left-hand corner of the page toward you. What is the vertical strand layout? What value range? Prints or solids?

What is the horizontal strand layout? What value range? Prints or solids?

What type of strands were used? How does the change in them for the fringe suit the autumn theme? How does the length of strands differ across the mat? Why?

This piece was plaited over a triangular board. What do you think is on the other side? What technical problems had to be solved? How did I do this? Plait a triangle of your own over wood or card. Choose your own theme, colors, and prints. Hang it where the wind twirls it around and ripples the fringe.

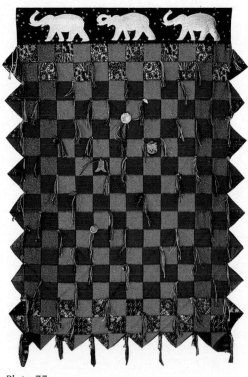

Plate 77.

Chapter Six
IT LOOKS LIKE PIECEWORK, BUT...

Are you ready to take your knowledge and your courage in both hands and plait a quilt? You can do it the easy way, as I did for "Plait Time in the Melting Pot." Seven blocks of ironed-over edge strands combine with two blocks of padded appliqué on black backgrounds. These nine blocks are joined by black sashes in the usual way for sashed quilts. A black border with heavy quilting frames them.

To make blocks all the same size, I ironed strands over the card guide. (Refer to Chapter 2.) Eleven strands one inch wide make a block approximately 12 inches square.

When I asked for quilt blocks instead of mats secured with fusible web, two problems arose. How could I stabilize the block for sashing? How could I quilt a patchwork of strands not stitched together?

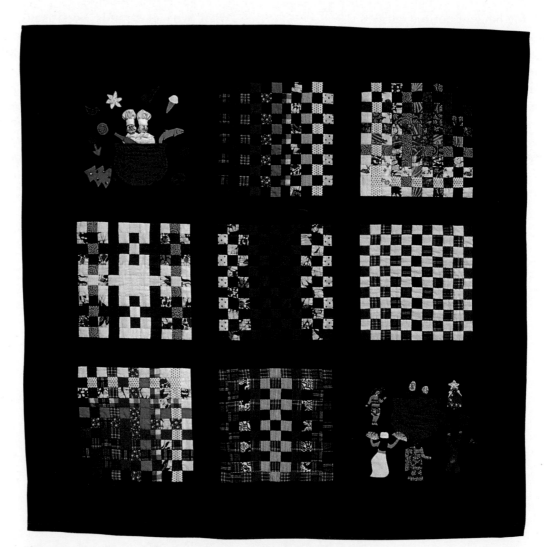

Plate 78. "Plait Time in the Melting Pot – Aotearoa Stew Retains Its Flavours," 53" x 53", celebrates culture-sharing in New Zealand (Aotearoa). At upper left, recent ministers of finance stew up contributions of immigrants from Europe and Asia. Meanwhile, women, carriers of culture, share their songs and dances. Like the plaited strands, each nationality retains its character as it helps build the new pattern. Suddenly the macho rugby players realize they are not being worshipped, but invited to join the dance as ordinary contributors. ©1988 Shari Cole.

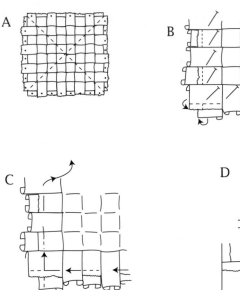
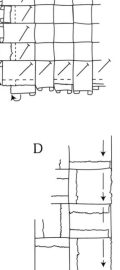

A

B

C

D

Figure 10 A – D.

↖— sash under block

dle batting. Baste as usual, being sure not to distort the plaited areas.

Beginning near the center of the quilt, stitch a few horizontal rows. Then rotate the quilt and stitch vertical rows, with those near the center done first. When crossing the sashes and border, use a normal quilting stitch. Plates 79 and 80 and Figure 11 show the special quilt appliqué stitch combination that I use within blocks. I quilt with the work spread on a table instead of a hoop or frame.

Plate 79.

Plate 80.

PREPARING IRONED-OVER EDGE BLOCKS FOR SASHING OR FRAMING, Figure 10 A – D

A. Measure the sides of the plaited block, and across the center in both directions. Adjust the strands as needed to equalize the measurements. Baste the block diagonally, crossing at the center.

B. Move the pins from the ends of the strands to the center of each horizontal and vertical outside row. Unfold the seam allowances of the outside edges. Dashed lines on the diagram represent the creases of these unfolded seam allowances.

C. With contrasting thread easily seen, baste the crossing strands to the unfolded outside strands, exactly on that crease. One stitch per crossing strand will do. These mark your machine stitching line.

D. Remove pins. Trim the block to ¼" outside the stitching. Assemble rows of blocks with short sashes as for any sashed quilt. Pin the raw edges of sashes to the raw edges of blocks, right sides together. Machine stitch, with the block uppermost so that you can make sure strand edges remain folded at the seam. Remove basting from edges, but not the cross-center basting.

QUILTING THE IRONED-OVER EDGE STRAND QUILT

Layer backing, batting, and assembled top as for any quilt. Choose a lightweight, easy to nee-

A. Quilt one stitch *beside the folded edge* of the parallel strand, down through crossing strand, batting, and backing, and up again (Plate 79).

B. Now appliqué one invisible stitch inside the fold of the parallel strand. Repeat A and B, alternating quilt and appliqué stitches. Four sets to the inch is adequate, six exceptional (Plate 80).

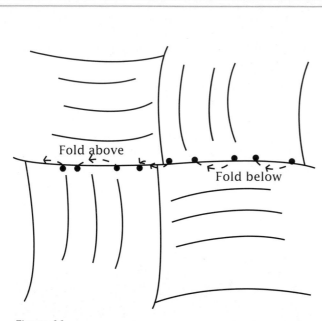

Figure 11.

C. At each intersection lace strand edges together so that no gaps appear. Here the folded edge changes from below to above, or from above to below. You must switch your appliqué stitch and the location of your quilt stitch to match. In Figure 11 the dashed arrows are stitches through the fold. The needle goes down at one dot and up through the next.

With practice you can combine the two stitches into one movement similar to appliqué blind stitch. If you enjoy hand stitching, the quilt appliqué block method provides speedy rewards.

My new solution generated a new problem – large, somewhat crooked stitches on the back of the quilt. What did I have to do? I backed this quilt with plaid. No one notices the stitches. This taught me that print backings are more fun than plain backings, so I use them often.

BEYOND THE BLOCK

Playing with blocks is just a beginning. Let's ask for more:

1. How long can ironed-over edge strands be?
2. Can we change fabrics in mid-strand and hide that join?
3. Can we plait directly over batting and backing already pinned to the board?
4. Must all quilts contain batting?
5. Do gently used folded edges need to be stitched?
6. Can we machine quilt ironed-over edge strands?

What problems do these questions generate? What can we do about them? Use the following suggestions as they suit your needs, or devise your own solutions:

A. Strand length is mainly limited by practicalities of the weaving set-up. My largest board measures five feet by four feet. Sometimes I work standing up with the board on the cutting table. For seated work space I lay the board on a low table. Any size will do, as long as I can reach the working area from the commencement edge or either side.

My boards are flannel-covered for fabric try-outs on the wall. For weaving I pin a flannel-backed plastic tablecloth over the flannel, its extra length hanging off the fourth edge (Plate 81). This solves three problems.

For a guide to straight sides, I fold the left and right edges of the plastic to the intended size of the mat. The plastic also resists the needle when I baste, tack intersections, or tie tassels. I never sew my project to the flannel board by mistake.

Sometimes I *do* pin it to the plastic cover on purpose. If a mat is to be very long, I start it as usual. When the reach becomes difficult I baste the finished portion, then pin it to the plastic in a few places. I fold mat and plastic together for about three turns of nine inches, bringing the working row to within a foot of my seated position. Don't let the finished portion of a mat hang off the edge. This pulls the strands (Plate 82).

What if you wanted a plaited bedcover? Could you use the whole mattress as a pinboard? I haven't tried this yet, but it sounds possible.

Plate 81.

Plate 82.

B. There's no reason not to piece different fabrics together in one strand. Joins may show if you have to readjust positions after weaving.

C. I have plaited several small quilts directly onto light batting and backing pinned to the board. I bound the edges of some by folding the harmonizing print backing to the front after trimming strand ends. Direct plaiting means basting only once. Because batting is springy, pin within rows as well as at row ends, as needed.

Plate 83.

D. The quilts-without-batting question concerns words rather than reality. We can plait bedcovers directly onto backing, or construct them from tubes and tassels with no backing. If we call them coverlets, we're covered.

E. For a wallhanging or other decorative item seldom washed, ties or a few stitches at intersections suffice to stabilize. Escaping batting is another matter. For a firm filling without quilting, use flannelette or blanket material. Pre-

shrink blankets by washing twice in barely warm water, as you would wash the project itself.

F. Machine stitching can add a design element, as for the badges and blouse. In use, ironed-over edge strands may uncrease. Stitching must cross them many times.

Barbara Johannah has devised a machine technique called "continuous curve." Instead of following the ditch, the stitching line crosses each intersection diagonally, then curves gently down the patch to the next intersection. This method is perfect for plaited patchwork.

Stitch on *top* of the fold, instead of on the ditch side, securing the raw edge under the fold. Invisible nylon thread on top creates a rippled effect especially attractive on pastels. Begin at one end of a row and meander its entire length.

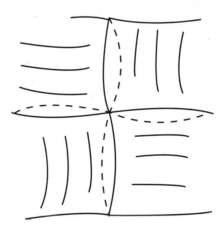

Figure 12.

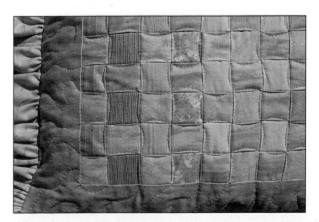

Plate 84. In this cushion cover, ironed-over edge strands are partly fused to backing. Both are layered over batting and lightweight backing. A #80 needle and matchmaker foot were used to quilt.

Without interrupting the stitch line, move up to the next row along the ditch of the border or binding. Alternately, meander into the border and back again as in Plate 84.

THROWING A CURVE

I hear you asking subversive questions out there. "Is plaited patchwork limited to rectangles and triangles? Do all strands have to have straight edges?" The obvious answer, no, raises another question. How and when do we turn the edges of curved strands? I find the following curved strand technique a joy to plait and appliqué.

Verticals are normal ironed-over edge strands. Horizontals curve in waves.

Plate 86. *The needle strokes the raw edge under a short distance ahead of the last stitch, while the other thumb holds the fold until stitched. Turn as you go, clipping inward curves shallowly as needed. Never clip outward curves.*

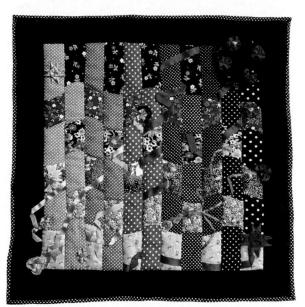

Plate 85. *"Starry Eyed Down the Garden Path," 16" x 16", symbolizes disillusion and dissolution when people naively depend on promises never intended to be kept. Hearts and bouquets connect to funeral flowers, and carefully constructed plaits fall apart as morning in the garden sinks to darkness. Thus embellishments of ribbon, lace, and beads emphasize the theme. ©1988 Shari Cole*

I plaited, basted, lifted, and framed this small quilt in the same way as the blocks for "Plait Time." Then I layered it with batting and backing and appliqué quilted. Beginning with the center horizontal row I turned and stitched the curved edges, one section at a time. Plate 86 shows the needle turn appliqué method.

End stitching where horizontals pass under

verticals. Shorten your appliqué stitch on curved edges by taking two appliqué stitches to every quilting stitch. In Figure 13 the horizontal strands are already quilt appliquéd. You can see that they do not meet at the intersection. Turning seam allowances for appliqué has caused this. Because the vertical strands, with their edges ironed over before plaiting, cover the entire surface, this is no problem. Because these flat horizontals cause little expansion, verticals are close together.

Quilt appliqué the verticals after you finish *all* horizontals. When you come to each intersec-

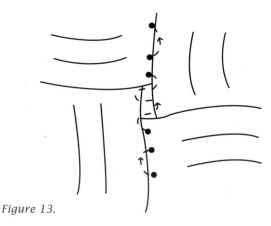

Figure 13.

tion, ladderstitch the two verticals together, then resume the usual alternating stitches.

TO BATT OR NOT TO BATT

Let's realize that needle turn quilt appliqué becomes clumsy when the thumb that holds the fold is blocked by a wad of fabric and batting. You can probably manage a project three feet wide if batting is thin. Beyond that, I would use backing only, for a fillerless coverlet.

A NOTE ON BASTING CURVED STRAND QUILTS AND COVERLETS

Baste in a line ½" from the top and bottom edges of every horizontal row, unless the strand is only 1½" wide, in which case a single row of basting is enough. After completing the quilt appliqué on horizontals, and before stitching verticals, remove row basting. You can then add any embellishments that pass behind the verticals, as in "Starry Eyed Down the Garden Path," Plate 85. Leave the basting at the top and bottom of the quilt, and at left- and right-hand edges until the border or binding is applied. Compare the appearance of the horizontal rows in Plate 87 with those in the finished quilt, Plate 90. After strand edges are turned, sections of the row float in a ground made by the verticals.

Plate 87.

EMBROIDERING A GOOD STORY

When Anne Pluck attended a four-day workshop in plaited patchwork, she set herself two goals – to make her own fabric for embroidery, and to use blue, a color she disliked. Her project in curved plaiting over batting became her "Voyage of Discovery" as she unified red horizontal sections floating in a navy ground by freely working embroidery stitches across the surface. Spiderweb, chain, herringbone, and cretan stitches bled red into blue and blue into red.

Plate 88. "Voyage of Discovery," 15" x 18", by Anne Pluck of Wanganui, New Zealand.

A SPECIAL OPPORTUNITY

Notice that Anne cut holes in some overstrokes, revealing the understrokes. She thus changed the balance of red and blue in some areas. Plaited strips give us a double layer of fabrics chosen for compatibility, and an opportunity to further counterpoint them by cutting away part of the top layer. Curved strands especially suit this reverse appliqué technique.

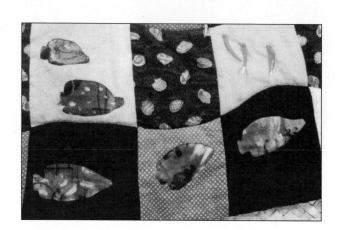

Plate 89.

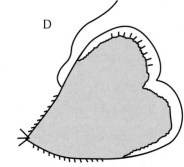

B

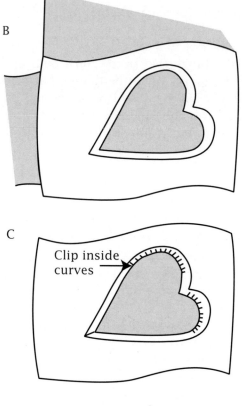

C

Clip inside
curves

These fish-shaped holes are not limited to underlayer fabrics. I inserted tropical prints resembling the markings of coral reef fish. Simple shapes are the key. I find inward curves and shallow points easiest to stitch in reverse appliqué. Geometric figures – diamonds, ovals, and triangles – complement curved plaiting, as do flowing freeforms.

BASIC REVERSE APPLIQUÉ

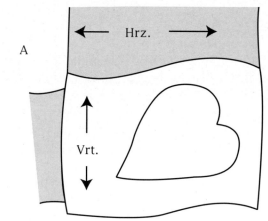

A

Hrz.

Vrt.

Figure 14 A.

D

Figure 14 B – D.

A. Draw the chosen shape on the top layer, in the exact finished size. Leave enough fabric *inside* the shape for seam allowance. *Outside* the shape, seam allowance needs tucking room. Avoid the raw edges of horizontals (print) *under* the verticals. If you don't draw well, cut simple paper shapes. Place them on the strand to check size. When it is right trim the paper *slightly*. Trace around it with hard pencil for light fabric, soap or white marker for dark.

B. Carefully pick up just the top layer of fabric, inside the shape, and snip through it. Cut *inside* the drawn line, leaving about ³⁄₁₆" seam allowance.

C. Clip inside *curves* not quite to the line, many times. Clip inside *points* once, to the line.

D. Roll the seam allowance under, far enough to just hide the drawn line. Needle turn appliqué, using a blind stitch. If your project is over batting, do not let the needle pick up the batting. Stitch fabric only. At inside corners there is no seam allowance. Take three overcast stitches, down through the same hole at the point, then up through the top fabric in a sunburst.

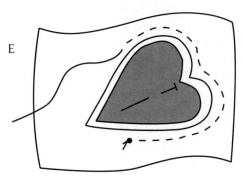

Figure 14 E.

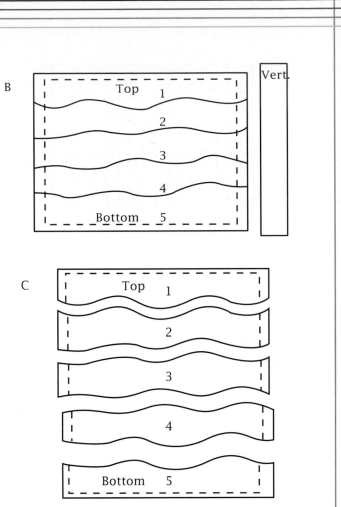

Figure 15 B – C.

For a different fabric showing through the hole, follow steps A and B. Use your paper shape as a guide to cutting the insertion fabric ¼" or ½" larger all around than the finished hole. Position and pin the fabric inside the cutout, making sure its edges extend well under the turning line. If possible, hold it up to the light to check this.

Baste outside the turn line, catching the insert but leaving room to turn the seam allowance under. Remove the pin. Clip and stitch as in steps C and D.

MAKING PATTERNS FOR CURVED STRIP PLAITING

Study the curves of "Starry Eyed" and "Voyage of Discovery." The bottom curve of each horizontal is the same as the top curve of the horizontal below it. This prevents horizontals from colliding at intersections. We cut horizontals from a paper pattern based on the size of the finished quilt.

A. Draw the finished size, represented in Figure 15A by the broken line. Add seam allowance to the *top* and *bottom* edges. Add takeup and seam allowances at the sides, which are the ends of vertical strands. Eight percent will do, four percent at each end, plus ½" at each end.

Freely draw or cut waves across the paper. Relate each curve to the one you drew before it – more extreme or less extreme. Remember that these strips lose seam allowance at the top and bottom during stitching. Draw them slightly deeper than you think you want. Number them from top to bottom.

B. Decide on the finished width of vertical strands. Hold sample strips over your pattern to test the effect of wider and narrower verticals. (See Figure 16.) Add 8% takeup allowance to the height of the pattern. Cut verticals that long.

C. Cut the horizontal pattern apart. Pin each piece to the fabric you intend for it. Cut out fabric around the edges of the paper. Leave the pattern piece pinned to it until you are ready to weave that strand in. That way you won't mix up strands or stretch them.

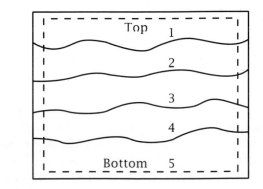

Figure 15 A.

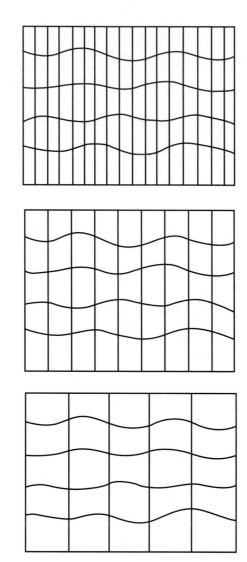

Figure 16. Changing the width of verticals changes the size, shape, and proportions of visible segments of horizontal strands. This affects the whole composition. Narrow verticals carry the eye up and down. Very wide verticals turn horizontals into waving ribbons.

Plait your project as you would any ironed-edge block. Finish as described earlier.

WHEN IS WASTE NOT WASTE?

In plaited strips and tubes, only the narrowest strands use less fabric than conventional piecing, for the amount of pieced surface on both sides. Somewhere between half and one inch you break even. At two-inch strand width, conventional piecing requires much less, but you have reached reverse appliqué capability.

Wide-strand plaited patchwork does take more fabric. Trade-offs are:

•Plaiting contains a bias toward unity. Designing is easier.

•Plaiting gives special opportunity for reverse appliqué, pockets, and interwoven embellishments.

•Routine work of cutting, machining, and ironing come first. The reward of watching beauty emerge in the weaving comes after, in a massive dose.

•Construction is often faster than conventional piecing and quilting.

•Batting is optional. These multiple layers are firm enough for bedcovers and garments.

THINK SMALL

I suggest you start with a small project in curved strand plaiting, with reverse appliqué over thin backing and batting. Don't reduce the *width* of strands in my sample Halloween quilt below (Plate 90) – reduce their *number*. Larger reverse appliqués are easier to stitch. You might plait and appliqué three horizontal rows, perhaps houses, pumpkins, and cats. Look for simple designs throughout the book that can be used for appliqué and reverse appliqué. Or choose your own seasonal theme – Christmas trees or Valentine hearts. Use this undemanding project to get the feel of handling the layers of appliqué and appliqué/quilting.

Sharp inward points are not practical in reverse appliqué. They leave you no seam allowance for some distance. *If you want sharp forms,* like the autumn leaves, apply them as *regular appliqué.* Again I caution you about horizontals crossing under verticals. The people, trees, and other figures do not have their feet on the ground because some of them would step off the edges of their underlays. Where the underlay is a vertical, there is no problem but you still need room to tuck the seam allowance under.

TECHNICAL NOTES TO ADAPT
FOR YOUR OWN CURVED STRAND PROJECT

Try these measurements for your small project. When that way of working becomes easy, you can make the coverlet with backing, but no batting. This is a very large piece for this technique, so be conservative in your initial commitment to reverse appliqué.

Measurements: 11 Vrt cut 4" wide (3½" after edges ironed). Hrz pattern is cut freehand, each

Plate 90. "Hallowe'en – Beggars' Night," 39" x 42", Shari Cole, 1994.

buy twice as much of the most expensive fabric in town for the wide strands of "Why the Moon Man Fishes the Sea" in Plate 91. Yes, I did design the coat as curved strip plaiting with appliqué and reverse appliqué. Yes, it does answer the questions you are probably asking:

"Do verticals have to be strictly vertical?"

"Do the outside shapes of plaited quilts have to be rectangular?"

Verticals are descending moon rays, widening toward the bottom. Horizontal currents undersea weave in and out of the rays, curving around the shaped bottom of the coat. Their values darken with depth.

All this is coded on the master pattern I drew, assisted by a yardstick. It looks much like the simple patterns in Figures 15 and 16 except for its outside shape and the letters and numbers in every section.

But instead of cutting strands, I traced a second heavy paper pattern, with all the letters and numbers, and cut it up for templates. I hand pieced curves and machine pieced straight lines, and appliquéd and reverse appliquéd. The coat and dress took six weeks of full-time work. It was worth it.

row beginning and ending the same width. When plaiting is complete, compare the measurements of top, bottom, sides, and across centers before basting the finished piece. Make adjustments where needed.

Design considerations: Limited number of fabrics for Hrz and Vrt. Layout is grouped in value sets. Lighter brighter fabrics are for accent only. All paper shapes for appliqué are placed, pinned, and viewed after all strands have been stitched. Outlines are drawn, but papers are left pinned as well, with notes if other fabrics are to be inserted.

FLYING TIME – DESIGNING AS IF...

Tradeoffs notwithstanding, I was not going to

Plate 91. "Why the Moon Man Fishes the Sea," inspired by a childhood poem and night diving on the reef. ©1989 Shari Cole for Fairfield/Concord fashion show.

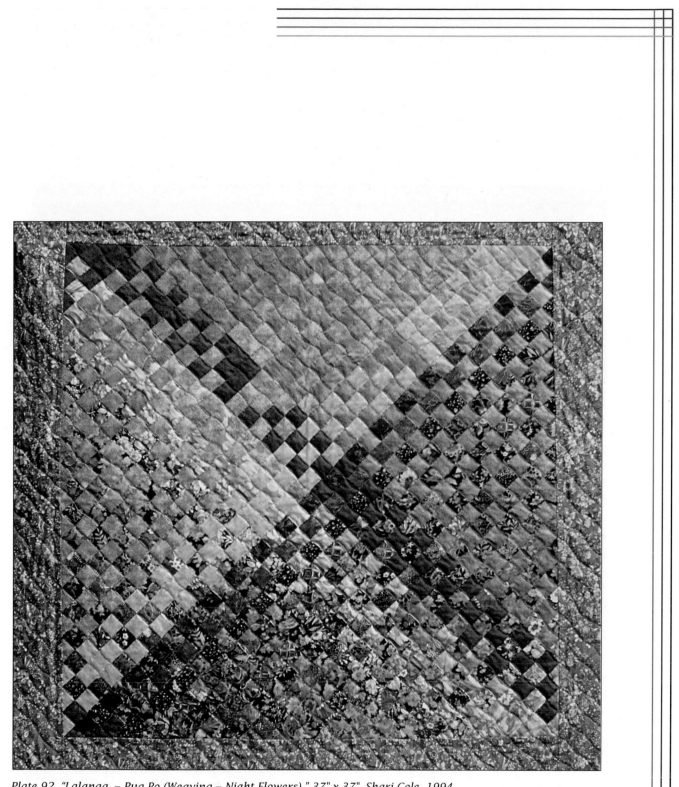

Plate 92. "Lalanga – Pua Po (Weaving – Night Flowers)," 37" x 37", Shari Cole, 1994.

Plate 93. "Autumn Taualuga," 37½" x 37½", Shari Cole. The third in the series of diagonal-weave quilts with value changes washing color across the surface. Values shade from the center of the commencement edge, both in the left-pointers and the right-pointers. Extended ends of the strands form borders. Every strand changes in value. Hand-quilt appliqué gives a raised texture.

Taualuga is the plaited cover of the ridgepole of the roof, which completes and holds in place the thatching. Taualuga is also the last, most graceful dance, which completes and surpasses all dances before. In autumn, nature weaves a taualuga of colored leaves, which dance in turn their taualuga as they fall. The autumn of life is our time to weave, and to dance our taualuga.

Plate 94. "Pua Lalanga" (Flowers Woven), 39" x 39" ©1994 Shari Cole. The print border blurs the edge between the plaitwork and the wall, and reinforces the flower theme. The commencement edge is at the top, with the offset yellow strands suggesting the sun. Hand and machine quilted.

Chapter Seven
SKIPPING OVER THE OBVIOUS

You've taken horizontal checkerwork with regular-width strands about as far as it can go, and thrown a few curves as well. You've created pattern through value, then added color and print. Now we start over, at the fork of the road not taken.

Twillwork, pattern formed by skipping strands according to a plan, could fill a book by itself. However, the simplest patterns are the most useful in work with cloth. Twill is less stable than checker. Its long overstrokes tend to crowd. When you ask for the added texture and pattern of twill, you have to adapt your work methods.

•Take care not to crowd strands when plaiting. Maintain tiny spaces between strands on carryovers. The slack is taken up in the return to checkerwork.

•Use pins within rows to keep strands aligned.

•Choose techniques that stabilize:
Fusing or machine stitching to a base fabric
Quilt appliqué through a backing
Many tassel ties through tube plaiting
Invisible hand stitching in twill areas of mats

EXERCISES FOR EXPLORING TWILLWORK
I use twill in three ways:

1. As feature medallions placed symmetrically in a checker ground.

2. As "accidental" figures placed randomly in checkerwork.

3. As repeat patterns, with checker filling only the edges of mats.

Let's deal first with symmetrically placed figures, the most straightforward of traditional work. Prepare paper strips as dark, light, and a few medium tag sets, as for Chapter 3.

Pin a 15-strand set-up of light verticals to your weaving board. This basic diamond medallion needs an odd number of strands for centering. Raise *even* numbered verticals. Lay in and weave one dark horizontal. Add two more rows of checker, for a base of three rows. Mark the center vertical (8 of a 15 strand set-up).

Twill diamonds begin with the center strand. *We develop twill pattern either by raising verti-*

Plate 95.

cals that would be lowered in checker, or by leaving verticals down that would be raised in checker. Study the *small* handbag in Plate 10. The light diamond at left has light *verticals* left *raised.* The dark diamond at right has dark horizontals passing over *verticals* left *down.*

The contrasting cross at the center of each diamond is made by raising strands that were down, for a short trip over one and over three rows. Besides adding interest, these crosses secure the long overstrokes. No strand skips over more than five rows.

Study the large handbag. Light patterns are vertical overstrokes. Dark patterns are horizontal overstrokes. Notice how strands from the bottom set are brought up to secure long overstrokes as part of the pattern.

Let's plait a dark diamond like the one on the small handbag. It's easier to develop pattern by leaving verticals down, because you can *see* the horizontals skipping over as you add them. Therefore, start the diamond in a row in which its center vertical is already down. Compare Plate 95 and your practice mat. You began by raising even numbered verticals. Vrt 8 is down in even numbered rows. Start the diamond in Hrz row 4. Count that single dark checker stroke over Vrt 8 as the first row of the diamond.

1. Raise odd Vrt. Lay in Hrz 4 as for ordinary checker.

2. Leave Vrt 8, the center Vrt, *down* as you weave the rest of the row in checker. Lower odd Vrt and raise even Vrt. This gives you 3 Vrt down at center (Plate 96).

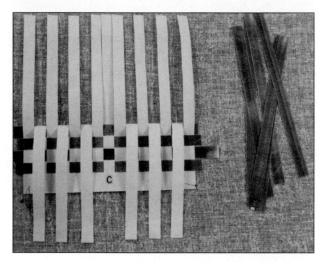

Plate 96.

3. Lay in Hrz 5. It skips over the 3 Vrt. Now leave 3 center Vrt down. Weave the rest of the row as usual, lowering even Vrt and raising odd Vrt. This gives you 5 Vrt down at center (Plate 97).

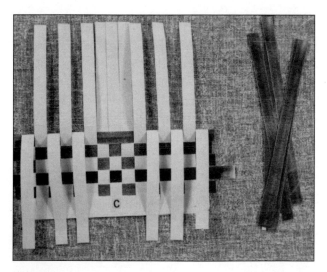

Plate 97.

4. Lay in Hrz 6. Leave the 5 center Vrt down. Finish the row as usual, odd Vrt down, even Vrt up. This gives 7 Vrt down at center. It's time to introduce the center cross (Plate 98).

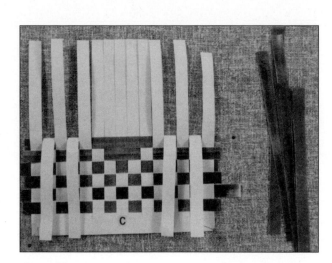

Plate 98.

5. Raise the center Vrt (Vrt 8). Lay in Hrz 7. We are going to change the center cross slightly, making a *checker cross* for interest and stability (Plate 99).

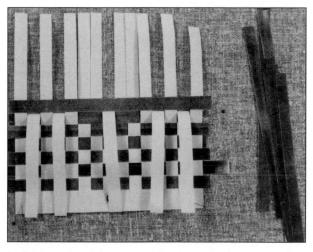

Plate 99.

6. Lower the center Vrt (Vrt 8). Raise the Vrt on each side of it (7 and 9). Leave Vrt 5, 6, 10, and 11 down. Weave the ends of row 7 as usual, lowering raised Vrt 2, 4, 12, 14, and raising 1, 3, 13, and 15. This expands the diamond to 9 spaces – a cross of 3 in the center and an over-stroke of 3 at either side. In Plate 100, *Vrt 4 has not been lowered yet.* The figure looks lopsided. With symmetrical twill diamonds, you can check for mistakes by looking to see that left and right sides of the figure are equal. If they are not, don't lay in the next horizontal until you find and fix the problem. (Be sure that *your* Vrt 4 is lowered before going on.)

Plate 100.

Plate 102.

7. Lay in Hrz 8 and lower all verticals to look at the pattern. This is the horizontal center of the pattern (Plate 101). From now on we *decrease* the pattern. Hrz row 9 copies 7, 10 copies 6, and so on.

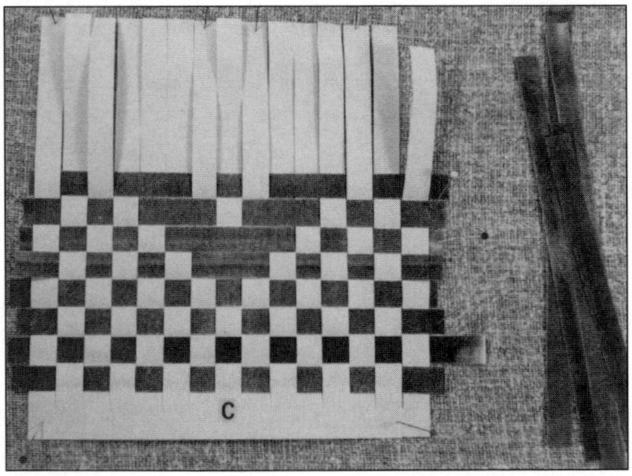

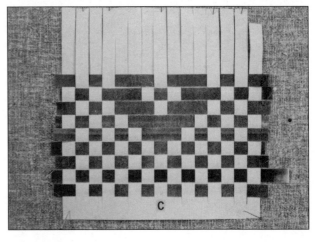

Plate 103.

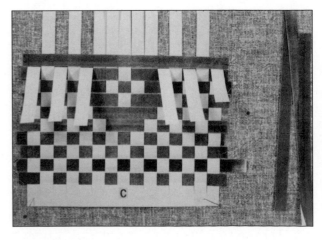

Plate 101.

8. To decrease in Hrz row 9, raise Vrt 2, 4, 12, and 14, as you did to open row 7 (Plate 99). For the last arm of the cross raise Vrt 8 (Plate 102).

9. Lay in Hrz 9. To see the pattern developing correctly, lower the raised strands. Rows 9 and 7 match (Plate 103).

10. Hrz row 10 decreases again, matching row 6. Raise Vrt 1, 3, 5, 11, 13, and 15. Lay in Hrz 10 (Plate 104).

Plate 104.

11. Leave 3 Vrt down at center as you return the rest of the row to checker for row 11. It matches row 5 (Plate 105).

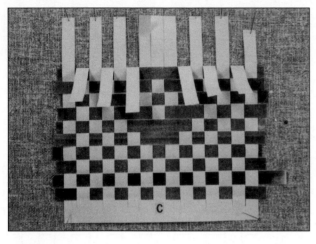

Plate 105.

Plate 106.

12. Lay in Hrz 11. Open the row for Hrz in checker. Vrt 8 stays down to finish the pattern. Row 12 matches row 4 (Plate 106).

13. Lay in Hrz 12. Weave the row and add three more rows of checker to complete a balanced mat with a diamond centered in a square (Plate 107). My practice mat ran out of vertical length on row 14, but you can see that 15 rows centers exactly. In the islands, weavers approximate right and left balance and worry less about centering up and down. You may prefer the pic-

ture-framing convention of a wider margin at bottom than at top, depending on the purpose of your project.

Turn the mat over and note the reversal of values. On the back, the verticals left down now

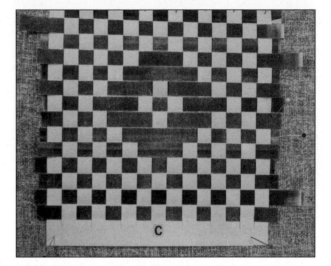

Plate 107.

skip over the horizontals. In tube plaiting this gives true reversed pattern, light dominant on one side, dark on the other.

An Exercise to Do by Yourself

Lay out the same practice set of 15 Vrt. Weave 2 rows of checker. Open the third row with Vrt 4 and 12 left down instead of raised for their normal checker strokes. (Did you begin by raising even numbered Vrt?)

Lay in Hrz 3. Raise all odd numbered Vrt. Yes, Vrt 4 and 12 remain down. Lay in Hrz 4. Lower all strands and look at the pattern you have made – two dark crosses set in checker and centered on Vrt 4 and 12.

Now look at Plate 96, the twill row open for Hrz 5. Weave your own diamond by following Plates 96 through 99. Stop increasing with Hrz 7 as the widest row. You will use one square, not a cross, to secure the center of the diamond.

Now weave row 7 in so that row 8 will *decrease*. It will match row 6. Figure out how to decrease this diamond one row at a time back to checker. Work two more crosses above, and fin-

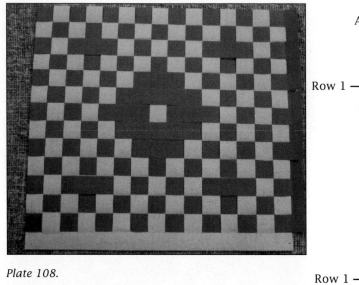

Plate 108.

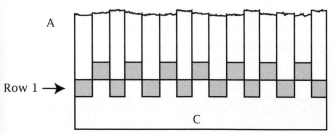

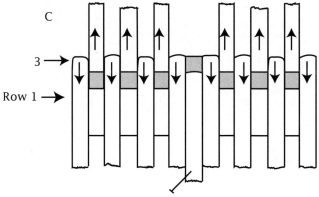

ish with a row of checker. Compare your mat with Plate 108.

Play with these possibilities. Can you make a diamond with a center cross but only two skips on each side of it? At which row does the one in Plate 109 start?

Plate 109.

Both copying and experimentation lead to understanding. Again prepare a 15-strand set-up for the diamond. Follow Figure 17 A – I, for a diamond formed by *raising* extra verticals.

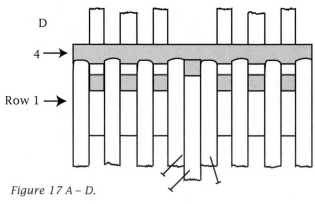

Figure 17 A – D.

72

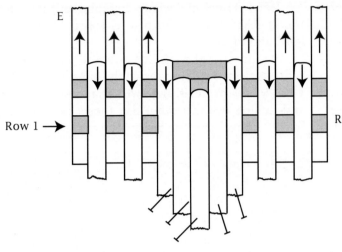

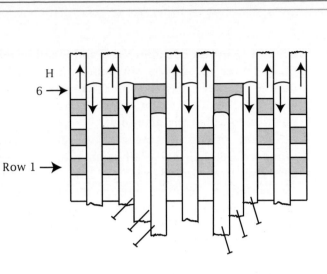

E

Row 1 →

H

6 →

Row 1 →

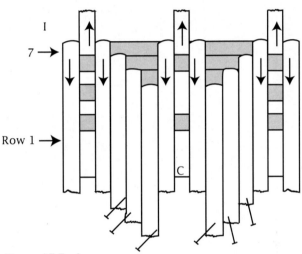

I

7 →

Row 1 →

C

Figure 17 E – I.

F

5 →

Row 1 →

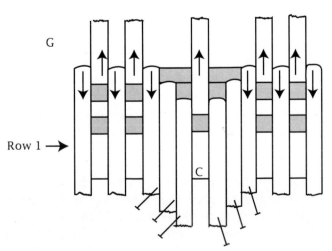

G

Row 1 →

C

A. Weave two rows of checker, even number Vrt raised in row 1.

B. Open the row for Hrz 3. The center Vrt is raised in this row. Leave it raised, with a pin to remind you.

C. Lay in Hrz 3. Close row 3, except for Vrt 8, as you raise odd Vrt for Row 4.

D. Leave the center and two companion Vrt raised (7, 8, 9). Pin them. Lay in Hrz 4.

E. Close row 4 as you raise remaining even Vrt for row 5. Pin Vrt 6 and 10 back and leave them raised.

F. Lay in Hrz 5. Note that it now passes behind 5 Vrt (6, 7, 8, ,9,10) without support. Let's add the center pattern.

G. Release the center pin and lower Vrt 8. Lower all even Vrt not pinned. Raise the remaining odd Vrt (1, 3, 5, and 11, 13, 15). Pin 5 and 11 in the raised position. They widen the basic diamond as you fill the center.

H. Lay in Hrz 6. Unpin Vrt 7 and 9 and lower them. Lower all odd Vrt not pinned. Raise Vrt 8 for the checker cross at center. Raise remaining even Vrt 2, 4, 12, 14. Pin 4 and 12 in the raised position to widen the diamond.

I. Lay in Hrz 7. Lower all raised Vrt not pinned (2, 8, 14). Raise all remaining verticals emerging from *under* Hrz 7 (1, 3, 7, 9, 13, 15). The pattern is complete through the center row. (Since it began in Hrz row 3, Hrz row 7 is the center.) Lower all Vrt to see if your sample looks like Plate 110.

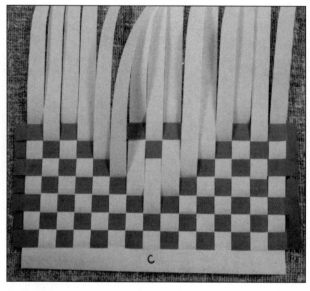

Plate 110.

Are your center verticals crowded? In twilling with raised verticals we tend to let horizontals pull the outside verticals toward the center. Keep outside edges straight, leave some ease, and lower all verticals every few rows to check pattern and tension.

Where do you go from here? Onward all by yourself on the road less traveled. I could lead you by the hand through the remainder of this twill figure, but that would add just one more pattern to your repertoire. Instead I return you to where you lowered verticals to look at the half diamond – Figure 17 I.

THREE PROBLEMS

I won't tell you how to solve these. Instead I'll show you the goals of the first two. The result of the third problem is your choice. Plait two more mats up to stage shown in Plate 110, then:

Mat 1: Finish the whole diamond and its central checker cross. Return to checker (Plate 111, left-hand mat).

Mat 2: Instead of finishing the diamond, return at once to checker (right-hand mat, Plate 111). View the resulting twill triangle sideways and upside down. I often use these half figures to fill "empty" checker spaces in compositions.

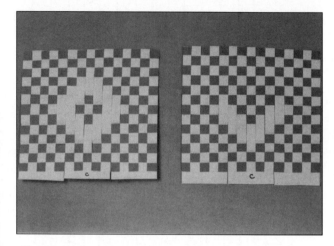

Plate 111.

Mat 3: Continue to *increase* the diamond. Increase the center cross to a triangular area of checkerwork. Make the diamond as wide as the mat allows. Carry it right off the edge if you like. Then decrease it in mirror image of the rows already plaited.

NOW PLAY

Devise your own patterns. Look at patterns on baskets and adapt them. Cut up junk mail and photocopies for their color and prints. Make an artist's book of patterns. Mount and frame patterns to cover a boring wall. Enjoy.

A TWINKLE OF TWILL

Balanced patterns are comfortable, and can be interesting as well. But I love the unexpected. Often I weave paper mats with planned color layouts, scattering twill figures randomly across them. These experimental mats become my graphed patterns for work in cloth.

I select fabric to represent each hue and value of the paper, not necessarily the *same* hue. A crosshatch blue paper may become a green jungle print. I use these plaited patterns for conventional pieced quilts as well as for plaited compositions.

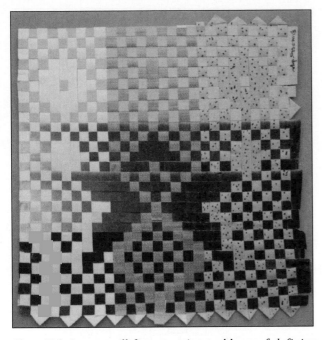

Plate 112. Large twill figures raise problems of defining the edges and still getting back into step with existing checkerwork. Study rows 5 through 11, from bottom. Extra twill strokes in the verticals separate dark horizontal twill from dark checker strokes.

Make your own larger experimental mats. Float twill figures in a checker ground. Balance the composition informally, with several small figures on one half weighed against a large figure on the other. Control the proportion of horizontal and vertical color by using the "verticals raised" or the "verticals left down" method of twilling. Include several colors in both sets of strands to see what happens when hue and value change within a figure.

Paint watercolor washes on paper to cut up for plaiting. These resemble the hand-dyed fabrics that you can buy, or you can paint with fiber-reactive dyes (Procion MX, Drimarine). More surprises await when you translate painted paper into painted fabric.

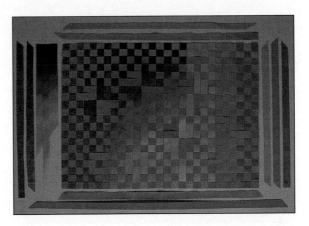

Plate 114. The papers used in this watercolor wash experiment are shown surrounding the mat. Trace their hue and value changes through the weave. Can you find five pairs of interlocking butterflies hidden among the hues?

For the sleeveless coat in Plate 115, I figured exact strand lengths to make the pattern fit. I cut yardage to that length and painted it before cutting strands. I knew that the coat back would occupy the centers of horizontals, with coat fronts and arrowheads using the strand ends. (Each double strand was pieced from two single strands, hence some dislocation of color fall.)

With a housepaint brush I applied fuchsia at center, yellow at either end, and a wavering transition area. Horizontals thus show pink at centers and yellow at sides. On the yardage for verticals, the supporting members of this colorful cast, I brushed a random blend of blue-purple and red-purple to complement the warmer hues.

Plate 113. Colored paper mats incorporating random twill figures preview the effect of hue and value at a distance. Overall contrast is greater in the left-hand mat. Six shades create 9 visual "blocks" from a value range of off-white to black. Each block contains a figure – cross, stairway, small diamond, or interlocking butterflies.

In the right-hand mat, 10 shades create 25 visual "blocks" from a lesser range of values. Crossing colors affect one another. Some twill figures cross boundaries and run off the edge. The crosses, stairway, and large diamonds are placed diagonally to draw the eye.

75

Plate 115.

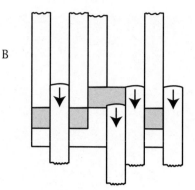

ONE MORE TWILL PATTERN

Both this coat and the pandanus mat in Plate 11 have a figure like interlocking butterflies. In the mat they form the overall repeat pattern. To plait the butterfly in a checker ground, follow Figures 18 A – G. You need a space of 8 Hrz and 8 Vrt, for a figure of 6 strands each way, plus a row of checker on all sides.

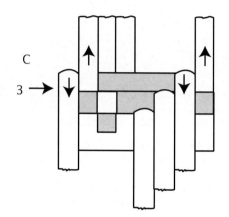

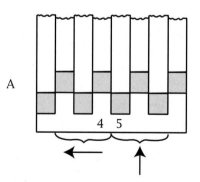

A. Work the first row checkerwork with even numbered Vrt raised, and a second row with odd Vrt raised. Close the row. Vrt 4 is an understroke, Vrt 5 an overstroke. Vrt 2, 3, 4 will form the understroke (lowered) set, and 5, 6, 7 the overstroke (raised) set in the first *half* of the figure. Then they reverse.

B. Raise Vrt 2, 5, 6, 8. This pattern is not symmetrical, but counterpoint. Strand positions reverse in the two halves, so it will not look balanced as you work the steps.

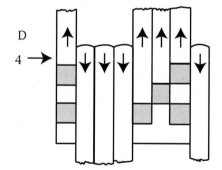

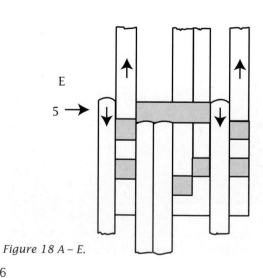

Figure 18 A – E.

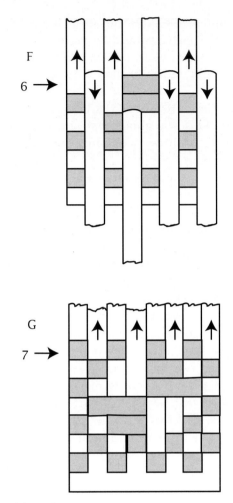

Figure 18 F – G.

C. Lay in Hrz 3. Lower Vrt 2 and 8. Leave 3 and 4 down. Leave 5 and 6 up. Raise 1 and 7.

D. Lay in Hrz 4. Lower Vrt 1, 5, 6, 7. Raise 2, 3, 4, 8.

E. Lay in Hrz 5. Lower Vrt 2 and 8. Leave 5 and 6 down. Leave 3 and 4 up. Raise 1 and 7.

F. Lay in Hrz 6. Lower 1, 3, 7. Leave 5 down. Leave 4 up. Raise 2, 6, 8.

G. Lay in Hrz 7. Lower all raised Vrt to see the completed figure, as in Diagram G. Then return to checker by raising the understroke strands – 1, 3, 5, 7. Lay in Hrz 8 and close the row to finish.

REPEAT PATTERNS

Next let's explore the simple idea of one strand up, two strands down in repeat twill. Lay out three identical mats in paper, this time using medium and dark for verticals, light for horizontals. Layout: Vrt: 3M, 3D, 3M, 3D, 3M. Hrz: 15L.

Mat 1: For Hrz row 1, raise only the first strand in each vertical value group of three strands. Leave the other two Vrt down. (That is, raise Vrt 1, 4, 7, 10, 13.) Lay in Hrz 1. Lower all Vrt.

For Hrz row 2 raise the second Vrt in each group (2, 5, 8, 11, 14). Lay in Hrz 2. Lower all Vrt. See the stairsteps?

For Hrz row 3 raise the third Vrt in each group (3, 6, 9, 12, 15). Lay in Hrz 3 and close the row. Repeat this sequence, raising first, second, then third Vrt in each group for the next 12 rows.

Once established, this twill pattern of over one, under two repeats in both horizontals and verticals. If you don't believe that, turn the mat on its side and look again. Now turn the mat over. What happens to value relationships on the back? You have plaited a two-faced pattern.

Mat 2: Now use this sequence of raised Vrt in each value group for 15 rows: 1st, 2nd, 3rd, 2nd, 1st, 2nd, 3rd, 2nd, 1st and so on. Compare this mat to the first one. How does the progression of twill overstrokes differ? How does the visual relationship between value groups of squares differ?

Mat 3: Use this sequence of raised Vrt in each value group: 1st, 2nd, 3rd, 2nd, 1st; 3rd, 2nd, 1st, 2nd, 3rd.; 1st, 2nd, 3rd, 2nd, 1st. Compare this mat with the first two. How does the twill progression differ? How does your eye group different values of squares? Check that you plaited the three mats correctly by comparing them with left-hand, center, and right-hand mats in Plate 116.

Compare the reverse sides of all the mats. In the second and third mats do vertical strands still pass over one horizontal and under two? Why has this happened? Do the dark vertical twill strokes form a regular pattern on the reverse sides of mats 2 and 3? Twill overstrokes increase the proportion of their color in the composition. What would you expect to see on the reverse side of the tube strand coat in Plate 115?

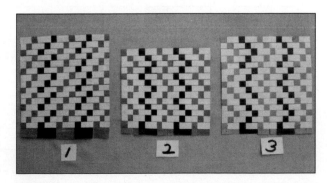

Plate 116.

A Digression

I mentioned using plaited paper mats as patterns for pieced quilts. If you want to piece one of these repeat twill patterns, analyze it in terms of Seminole. With two-inch finished squares in mind (2½" cut) for mat 2, you need:

Bands of double light (representing a stroke over two strands) with single dark (light strips cut 4½" to finish 4" wide, dark cut 2½" to finish 2" wide).

Bands of double light with single medium.

A band of single light with single medium (both cut 2½" to finish 2").

A few light squares, cut 2½" square to finish 2".

All cross-cuts are 2½" to finish 2". Figure 19 shows assembly.

You can make a safe, three-fabric quilt by counting the number of each type of segment needed for all the blocks. You can figure the exact yardage for cutting all those strips from the three fabrics.

I prefer the fun of uncertainty and surprise. Why do arithmetic when the same time can be spent solving problems? I would work from a heap of dark remnants and a heap of medium remnants. Maybe I would use the same light fab-ric throughout the quilt, but probably not. A mix of very pale pastels would be more interesting. I would cut strips, piece bands, and cross cut and join segments until it became a quilt.

INTRODUCING THE SUPERSTRAND

What can I say about a strand that presses its own seam allowances and looks like three strands in one? "Hooray!"

When you thought about the reverse side of the coat in Plate 115, did you expect dull purple dominating a composition much like the first side? Or did small clues in the arrowhead turns suggest that these are no ordinary tubes?

This coat reverses from twill in checker solid hues to a complex impression of stripes and prints, Plate 117. The seams of its tube strands lie within the print sides instead of at strand edges. Each tube contains firm, thin batting.

Figure 20 shows the construction in cross section. The two fabrics lie right sides together, with batting against the wrong side of the narrower fabric (the print). Cut batting and print to the desired *finished* width of strands. Cut solid fabric for the wrap-around strand width, *plus* ¼" for thickness allowance, *plus* four times the seam allowance.

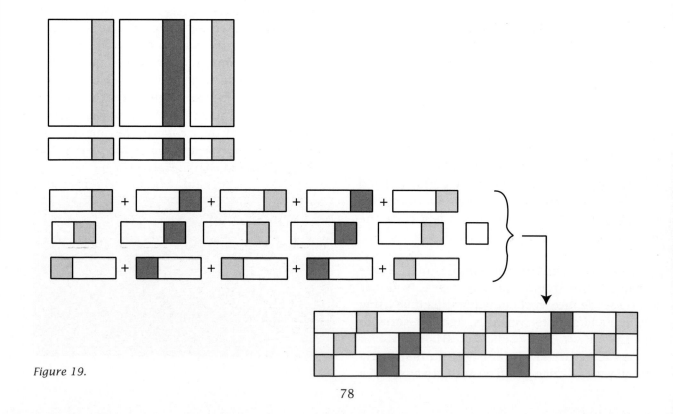

Figure 19.

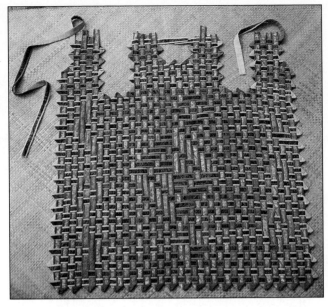

Plate 117.

Right sides together

A

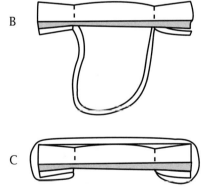

B

C

Figure 20.

For example, a one-inch strand requires:
Print strips 1" wide.
Batting strips 1" wide.
Solid color strips 1" + ¼" +(4 x ¼")=2¼" wide.
This includes a seam allowance of ¼". Because I like more of the print to show, I reduce seam allowance to the width of my presser foot with the needle in right-hand position (³/₁₆"). Thus I need ¼" less width in solid fabric (2" instead of 2¼"). Changing the seam allowance does *not* change the width of the batting and print fabric.

Plates 118 through 120 show how to stitch

and turn lapover strands. Compare them to the cross section diagrams. You can work with either the batting side down or the solid fabric down, whichever works better with your machine feed.

Place fabrics right sides together and batting on the wrong side of print fabric, *raw edges even* on the *stitching* side. Stitch. In Plate 118, the strand is folded back to show the positioning.

To stitch the second seam, again match the remaining raw edges of all layers. Fold excess solid fabric out of the way. In Plate 119 it protrudes from under the strand. Stitch. Do not sew across strand ends.

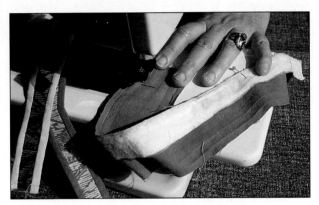

Plate 118.

Turn the tubes right side out, from between the *two fabric layers*. Turn very long strands through an opening in the stitching, near the center of one side, as for ordinary tubes. Flatten the turned tubes with the edges of batting and print at the sides, solid fabric wrapped around.

Plate 119.

79

Plate 120 includes a strand being turned, a strand with the first seam only sewed, a finished horizontal strand (yellow solid with overdyed purple print) and a finished vertical strand (purple solid with pink print overdyed yellow). Since the stripe effect of these strands depends on contrast, use a dark solid with a light print, or a light solid with a dark print.

Plate 120.

In the mat in Plate 121, navy contrasts with the yellow print in the horizontals, while yellow sets off a black and multicolor print in the verticals. On the reverse side, navy and yellow solids form a twill medallion and two crosses in a checker ground. Can you pick out these figures on the complicated-looking print side?

A WORD ABOUT FILLING STRANDS

I used an 80% cotton, 20% polyester batting (Fairfield Cotton Classic™) for the coat. I did not pre-rinse and tumble dry it as the manufacturer suggests for hand quilting. The original finish helps when rotary cutting strips. For the navy and yellow mat, I rotary cut strips from an old wool blanket, machine washed on the wool setting. Any washable, firm, thin filling will do.

Filled strands are heavy to wear. Because of their thickness, allow 15% takeup allowance and expect projects to expand sideways more than usual. If you use Niuean arrowhead layouts, allow extra for the turns. Twill areas need plenty of stabilizing.

You can experiment with lapover strands with no filling or very light flannelette filling. You will doubtless have to iron them, but this should be easier than ironing standard double-face strands.

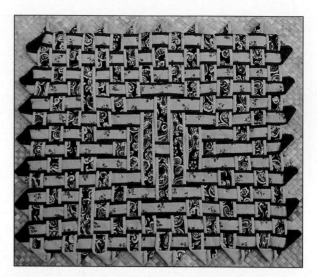

Plate 121.

DESIGNING FOR LAPOVER EDGE STRANDS

Aside from extra expansion of measurements during weaving, lapover strands present few problems used as single strands. Pin a paper pattern for a vest panel, perhaps the back, to your weaving board. Plait the panel and baste firmly around the stitching line of the pattern. Trim outside the stitching, leaving the seam allowance. Make the vest reversible. The woven panel can be worn with either side out.

Problems arise when we use lapover strands for those arrowhead turns they enhance so beautifully. That means joining strand ends every second row. Join with the print side up, on an overstroke:

1. Overlap the strand ends. Trim the overlap to 1". Unpick the stitching of one strand end to 1" from the end. On that strand end trim the batting back 1", to butt exactly with the end of the other strand. Trim just the corners of the solid fabric on the unpicked end (Plate 122).

2. Fold the solid fabric in to make a half-inch hem. Lay the second strand end into this "cradle," meeting the batting. Pin (Plate 123).

3. Slip stitch (appliqué) the back (solid color side) of the join. Don't bring the stitching around the sides yet, but leave the thread dangling for finishing later. Remove pin. As shown in Plate 124, unpick the stitching at the sides of the second strand end to a depth of ½". On the first strand end, trim the print fabric to overlap ½".

4. Fold ¼" hem in the print fabric you just trimmed. Tuck its sides under the solid fabric

Plate 122.

Plate 123.

Plate 124.

Plate 125.

Plate 126.

Plate 127.

lapovers. Slip stitch print to print, *catching the batting as well.* Now trim the lapovers of the strand end in the cradle back to the print hemline, reducing bulk (Plate 125).

5. Now continue the stitching of solid color fabric from the back of the strand, right around the lapover. With the needle, tease the outside solid fabric around the inside lapover as smoothly as possible. Restitch the lapover

by hand, far enough in each direction to prevent unraveling of cut threads. This join staggers the meeting of solid and print ends, reduces bulk, and gives the eye no straight line seam to focus on (Plate 126).

In garment construction, the need for pairs of strands makes design problems. For the coat I designed neck and arm openings in modules of two inches to use two one-inch strands.

Plate 128.

Plate 129.

Notice that the arrowheads on neck edges don't match those on armhole edges. Here I used the pandanus mat method of step-ups with one continuous strand. Since the shoulder seam needed conventional cutting, there was no need for equal edges (Plates 127 – 129).

PERMUTATIONS AND APPLICATIONS

You've learned some twill patterns and gained a basic understanding of twillwork. You know how to make the lapover strand. How can you combine these with other permutations and use them?

• Work frayed edge strips, ribbons, or ironed-over edge strands in twill on the wrong side of print fabric treated with fusible web. Cut it up for garments or border it with a quilted print frame for a wallhanging.

• Plait ironed-over edge strands in twill over batting and backing. Hand or machine quilt.

A PROJECT WITH SCOPE FOR YOUR OWN DESIGN

Here are technical notes for a lapover strand throw based on the navy and yellow mat. Choose your own fabrics, color layout, and twill figures. It will finish somewhere between 38" and 40" square.

Strip measurements for both Hrz and Vrt:

Prints and batting cut 1¼" x 44".

Solids cut 2½" x 44". Sew a test strand before cutting all solids. Your batting choice affects the fit.

Make 26 Vrt and join them into 13 double lengths before plaiting.

Do the same for 13 double-length Hrz. Each makes a strand pair.

Review Figure 6 for the arrowhead turn and Plates 48 through 63 for mats with points on all four sides. The mats in the photos have prairie points instead of arrowheads, but the principle is the same. Join strand ends by sewing rather than overlapping.

Stabilize points and twill areas with your choice of hidden stitches, buttons and charms, tied tassels, or whatever adds to the character of the piece.

FLYING TIME – CREATIVE WINDOW SHOPPING

Have you ever seen an original garment in a boutique and itched to examine it with camera, notebook, and tape measure to make your own version? You are welcome to analyze and make a coat or short vest based on "Sunset of the Weaver Wizards" for yourself. I've taken some notes for you.

Use Plates 115, 117 through 120, and 127 through 129, the other information I gave you about the coat and lapover strands, and the construction notes below. Count the rows. Calculate strand lengths. Experiment with paper mock-ups and graph paper. Remember that choice of material and your own plaiting tension affect expansion and takeup. This was a difficult undertaking, but I found it worthwhile for both the result and the process of exploration.

Notes: I used print and batting strips 1" wide, a scant ¼" seam allowance, and solid fabric strips 2⅛" wide.

I graphed a basic jacket pattern and drew the number of strands over it. Like most ethnic jackets this coat fits a wide size range – from 33" to 38" bustline. It is a rectangle mat with extensions.

The shoulder seam must be fitted to the person who will wear it, considering whether the garment underneath has shoulder pads.

Raw edges of the shoulder seam are on the solid color side of the coat. The seam is pressed open and tacked in that position. A rectangle of matching fabric appliquéd over the seam hides it. Shaggy tassels tied through the fabric give an epaulette effect.

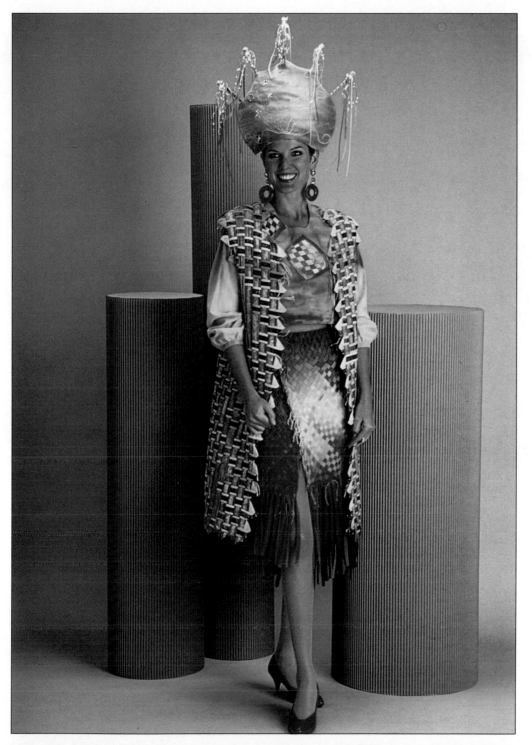

Plate 130. "Sunset of the Weaver Wizards," ©1992 Shari Cole made for the Fairfield fashion show. I had partly designed the garments and was painting fabric when I recognized the colors of the island sunset hour, and knew that every weaving method I would use came from what those elder women had taught me. The design and colors completed themselves from there.

Chapter Eight
LEAVING THE ROW
FOR THE WEAVER'S PATH – DIAGONAL WEAVE

Plate 131. "The Frog Printses of Night and Day Forest" wears a triangular shawl of diagonal plait-tube strands as she wanders through the forest blessing the animals with her magic sceptre. ©1992 Shari Cole for the "Statements" exhibition, USA.

Plate 132. A ribbon reticule in diagonal plait checker-work complements an island-style long dress with plait-ed ribbon insertions.

Note: LP's are shaded so you can follow them through the plaiting process.

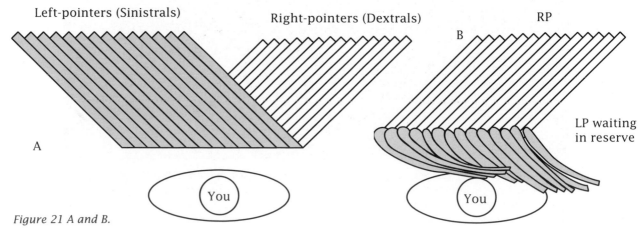

Left-pointers (Sinistrals)   Right-pointers (Dextrals)   RP

B

LP waiting in reserve

A

You

You

Figure 21 A and B.

ANOTHER ROAD NOT TAKEN

So far we've worked with horizontal and vertical strands. Thinking like quilters, we've assumed that diagonal set means turning horizontally constructed units on point. In Chapter 1 I mentioned coconut fronds as natural set-ups for diagonal plaiting. In lalanga when you ask for diagonal set, you think of strands pointing away from you at an angle, to left and to right. You sit at the commencement edge of the mat (Figure 21).

A set of right-pointing strands (technically called dextrals) lies against the weaving board. These will do the work of verticals. Raise and lower them to open the working rows.

On top of this right-pointing working set lies a set of left pointers (technically called sinistrals). These do the work of horizontals. Every right pointer has a left pointer partner. Lay left pointers into the open working rows. While waiting their turns, left pointers are swept back to the right and rear. They are like a pile of horizontals kept ready to lay in.

For convenience, we abbreviate these two sets as RP and LP.

Plaiting diagonally means constructing a mat on the bias, which presents problems:

• How do we secure the commencement edge?

• How do we begin the checkerwork?

• What happens when we run out of working strands (RP) at the left edge, and out of laying-in strands (LP) at the right edge?

• How do we finish the fourth edge?

• How do we stabilize those four bias edges? How do we stabilize the bias "fabric" we have plaited?

CIRCLING THE ISSUES

In our first project let's resort to modern technology to secure commencement and finishing edges – fusible web and the sewing machine.

Because we can't adjust strand spacing once the commencement edge is fused, let's use ribbons for flat strands with minimum expansion. Satin ribbon is good for its directional reflection of light. Let's stabilize the weave and complement the ribbons with a print fabric lining.

We'll evade the right and left edge question by not having any. A cylinder has no side edges. Coconut frond gardening baskets and ladies' handbags are cylinders with their bottom ends

closed. The lined ribbon reticule in Plate 132 is a closed-end cylinder.

You Need:

12 pieces of ⅝" wide ribbon cut 14" long in a light color for RP.

12 pieces of ⅝" wide ribbon cut 14" long in a darker color for LP.

Harmonizing print fabric for lining cut 12" x 9½", plus a strip 12½" x 2¼" for binding.

Silk cording for shoulder strap – 3 colors to braid if desired.

Fusible web, fine pins for satin ribbon.

Towel to roll for a form to plait over.

Procedure:

Apply a ½" wide strip of fusible web to the wrong side of the lining fabric along both 12" edges. Lay the lining fabric wrong side up on your weaving board, with the 12" edge parallel to the bottom edge of the board. Leave space at the bottom of the board for LP to lie in reserve.

As shown in Figure 22, place a pin ½" from the left edge of the fabric and ½" up from its bottom edge. The distance from there to the top edge is 9". Place another pin *at* the top edge, ½" from the left edge. Place the third pin at the top edge also, 9" to the right of the second pin. You have marked three of the four corners of a 9" square. The dotted line represents this square. Pin the lower-right corner of the fabric.

The half inch of fabric at the left is seam allowance for closing the cylinder. The webbed half inch at the bottom is for setting up right-

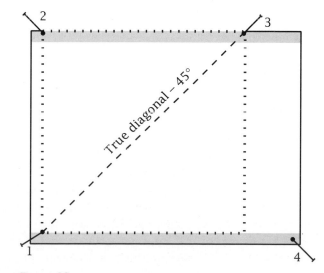

Figure 22.

85

pointer ribbons. The third pin marks the true diagonal of the 9" square (45°).

Refer to Figure 22 and Plate 133 as you lay in the first RP. The left-hand corner of its near end is close to the first pin. Its lower right-hand corner rests on the near edge of the fabric. Its left edge crosses the square diagonally and touches the third pin. Lay in all remaining RP parallel to the first, with their lower right-hand corners touching the near edge of the fabric. Leave a *tiny* space between strands. Fuse-baste the commencement edge. Remaining fabric at the right becomes generous seam allowance.

Plate 134.

Plate 133.

To set up the LP and establish the interlace start of checkerwork, work from the left end of the commencement edge. Lay LP 1 across RP 1 at right angles. Its left edge touches the pin. Its right edge makes a line straight across RP 1 and the bottom of RP 2. Its nearest corner extends off the edge of the fabric so that the strand is in contact with exposed fusible web. Pin LP 1 and RP 1 together through the board ½" up from the fabric edge, as in Plate 134.

Raise RP 1. Lay in LP 2, across RP 2 and the end of RP 3, to cover the second triangle of fusible web (Plate 135).

Pin as for LP 1. Lower RP 1. The first interlace stroke is done (Plate 136).

Raise RP 2. Lay in LP 3, across RP 1 and 3 and the end of RP 4, covering the third triangle of fusible web. Pin it. Lower RP 2. You now see the first stroke of the interlace framed as a diamond – the first step of the ala, the weaver's path (Plate 137).

Plate 135.

Plate 136.

Plate 137.

Continue raising one RP at a time and laying in the next LP until you run out of LP strips. (Count to make sure you have equal RP and LP.) Fuse the LP ends to the lining. Remove pins except for those at the corners of the fabric, (Plate 138).

Plate 138.

FOLLOWING THE ALA – A STRAIGHT PATH WHEN ALL ELSE SLANTS

Plate 138 shows the completed interlace, a horizontal row of diamonds parallel to the commencement edge. Polynesians call such a row the *ala* (or a similar word, depending on which language) meaning path or way. They diagonal-plait mats in sections instead of in rows as for hori-

zontal weave. By keeping the top line of the completed section (the ala) exactly parallel to the commencement edge, they control the shape and tension of the mat.

The *working row* slants from upper left to lower right. LP are laid into working rows. Look back at Figure 21 A. Tilt the book so left pointers become horizontals and right pointers become verticals. Now look at Figure 21B, LP swept back in reserve for laying in. The first working row at the left will begin and end with one LP overstroke. The last working row at the right will involve all RP with the last LP woven through. This leaves us with a plaited triangle and many loose ends. What do we do?

Instead of weaving every working row to its full length, we work a few strokes in each, then go to the next row. We work the same number of strokes in each row. The working rows march across the mat from the left to right, each ending in a diamond made by a right-pointer overstroke. Again, this row of diamonds is the ala. Ends of left pointers are left loose on top of right pointers after they emerge from under the ala diamond. When we finish the ala, we sweep loose left-pointer ends back in reserve for the next ala.

Plate 139.

Plate 139 shows the ribbon bag with a new ala partly woven (three diamonds across the top of the weaving). My finger points to the working row just plaited. My right hand lifts two RP to open the next row. Waiting LP are swept back at right.

How do we get from the interlace in Plate

138 to the second ala in Plate 139? Figures 23A – I show you. The left end of the mat remains incomplete until we close the cylinder.

A. With the interlace ala completed, your mat looks like Plate 138. Leave LP 1, 2, and 3 down. Sweep all other LP back, as in Figure 23A. Note that LP 1, 2, and 3 are already woven into working rows 1, 2, and 3 in plaiting the interlace.

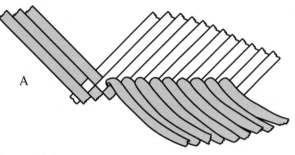

Figure 23 A.

B. Raise RP 1, the *understroke* nearest the waiting LP.

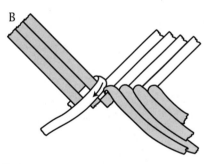

Figure 23 B.

C. Lay in LP 4 and lower RP 1. This is the fourth working row. Which strand should you raise next to continue the checkerwork?

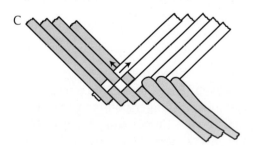

Plate 23 C.

D. Raise RP 2. Lay in LP 5.

Tilt the book, and your ribbon mat, to see this as raising Vrt 2 and laying in Hrz 5. What would you do next to close the fifth row?

E. Lower RP 2.

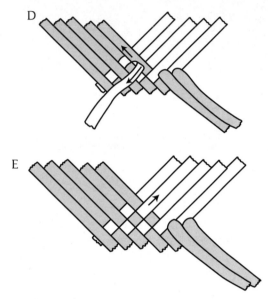

Figure 23 D and E.

F. How many RP must now be raised to open the row for the next LP? Raise them. Lay in the LP.

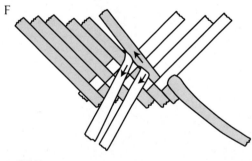

Figure 23 F.

G. Lower all raised RP. Which two RP will you raise next? We count the ala by the number of RP we raise for each working row as we work across the mat. Counting keeps us from raising too many RP and losing track of the ala. Make this an ala of "two up and two down." This means open each row by raising two RP. Close the row by lowering two RP as you raise two RP for the *next* row. You always raise the two *understrokes* closest to you (the bottom of the row). In Figure 23G we have only two RP understrokes (marked X). We have reached an ala of two up. I marked the diamond A.

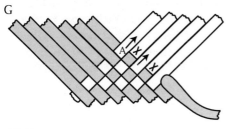

Figure 23 G.

H. Raise the RP. Lay in LP 7. Lower the two RP. LP 7 now passes over three RP by the time it emerges to *stay* on top, *above the ala.* For the next row we raise two RP *below the ala.* They are marked X in Figure 23 H. Always stay below the ala when raising RP. The diagram now shows all the strands of the ribbon mat, 12 LP and 12 RP.

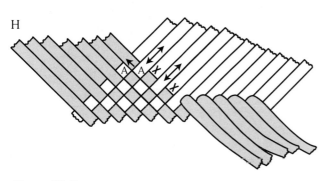

Figure 23 H.

I. Continue along this ala until it looks like Plate 139, with LP 8 and 9 woven into their working rows. Then complete the ala with no LP left in reserve. You have an interlace ala across the bottom (marked * in Figure 23 I) and a second ala two diamonds deep (marked A).

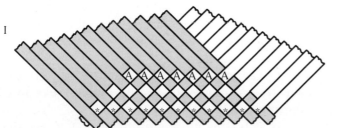

Figure 23 I.

GOING AROUND IN CIRCLES

Now baste the top of the ala to the fabric lining with a stitch through each point marked A in Figure 23 I. Be sure to catch that last RP stroke on the right, which is not yet framed as a diamond. Unpin the fabric and lift it from the board.

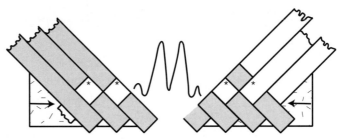

Figure 24.

In Figure 24, arrows indicate the matching points for sewing the lining sides into a cylinder. Measure the distance from right and left lining edges to these notches in the plaiting. Trim the wider edge of the lining to match the narrower, so that the seam allowance is the seam on both sides.

Fold the mat with the right side of the lining on the inside and ribbons on the outside. Pin through the matching points and again near the other end of the cylinder. Sweep loose ribbons away from the seam on front and back. Stitch the seam a *hair* outside the matching points, from commencement end to unfinished end of the cylinder. See Figure 25A.

Clip or pink edges to reduce fraying. Clip the corner at the unfinished cylinder end so the seam allowance doesn't block the fusible web. At the commencement end trim the seam allowance to ¹⁄₁₆" up to the matching point, then straight out to the edge, as shown in Figure 25 B.

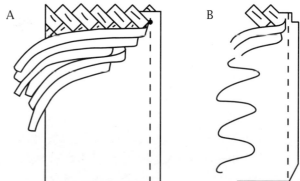

Figure 25 A – B.

Now fill in the cylinder plait up to the ala, following Figure 26 A – I.

A. Finger press the seam open. Tuck the seam allowance under the plaited area at the bottom. Insert a firmly rolled towel into the cylinder as a base for weaving. It should fit snugly, but don't pop that closely trimmed seam at the bottom. Insert pins through the top and bottom edges of the lining, straight into the towel, in several places.

Hold the cylinder up with the seam toward you so the ribbons dangle. Sweep the free LP back to the right, and the free RP back to the left. Your basting keeps the ala from coming undone on the back.

B. Lay the first six RP toward the right, into working position. The last diamond of the ala is at the top left, marked A. (The top of the cylinder is not shown in Diagrams B through H.)

In Figure 26B locate the first working row that you will open. To weave this up to the ala, you must raise three RP – two for the ala and one at the bottom for the interlace stroke that joins the left edge of the mat to the right edge, across the seam. (Find the incomplete interlace ends in Figure 23 I and Plate 138.) The RP understroke closest to you in Figure 26B belongs to the interlace.

C. Lift the three RP. Lay in the next LP.

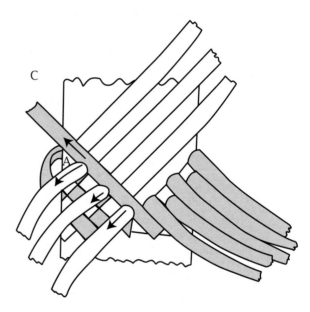

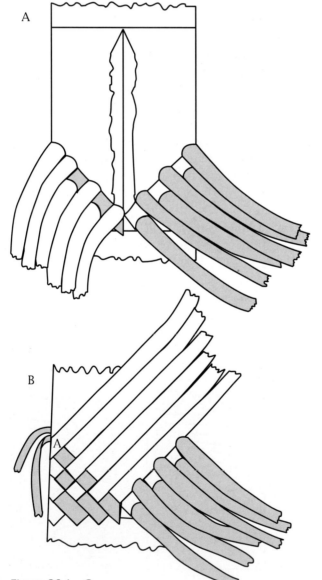

Figure 26 A – C.

D. Lower the three RP. In Figure 26 D, * indicates the final interlace stroke, and A indicates the top of the ala. Pin the ala, pushing the pin deep into the towel.

E. That LP now lies on top of the weaving after it emerges from the ala. Leave every LP you lay into a working row on top, until the ala is complete around the cylinder. Now we have only two understrokes below the line of the ala. Lift these and lay in the next LP.

F. Close the row. Pin the ala. Open the next row by raising the two RP understrokes that remain below the level of the ala.

G. Lay in the next LP. Close the row. Pin the ala. Notice that only *one* RP understroke now remains below the ala.

H. Raise the RP. Lay in the next LP. Close the row and pin the ala. One RP understroke remains.

90

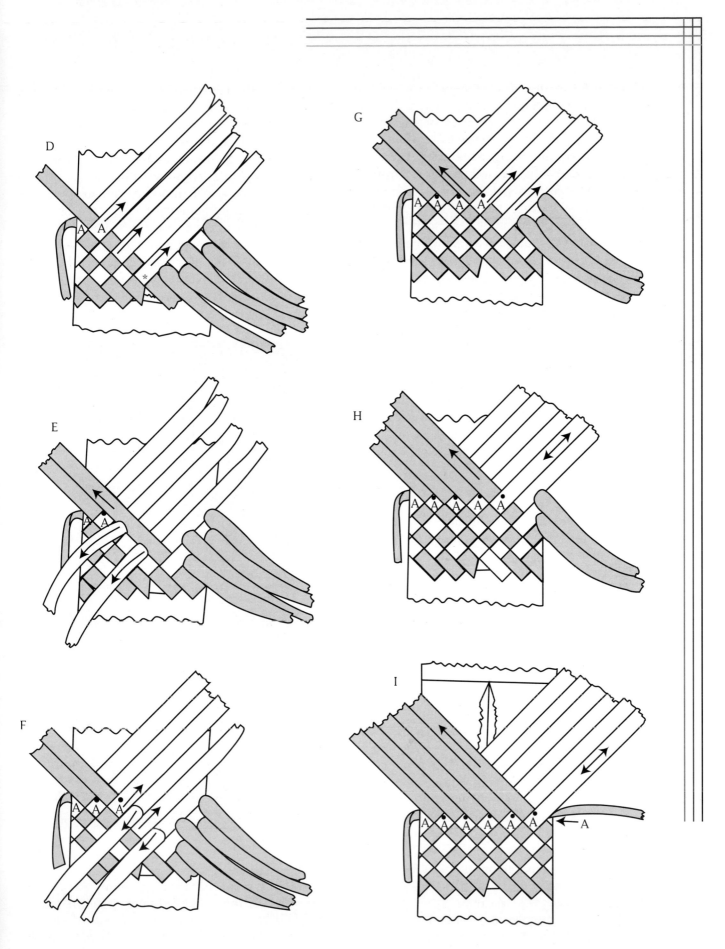

Figure 26 D – I.

All other RP are now incorporated in the ala.

I. To complete the ala raise the remaining RP. Lay in the last LP not already basted or pinned. Lower the RP. Pin this last stroke of the ala.

The arrow at the right indicates where your basting ended. That loose LP emerges from the ala. Lay it across to see the full ala completed. Note that the drawing shows the full cylinder and towel roll. A set of RP and LP are ready to begin a new ala. They are longer than shown here.

To finish this lined cylinder you need to keep in checker without missing any strands, until you reach the top of the lining. Even if you lose track of the ala, the top is marked out for you.

Standard procedure is to raise another ala of two up and two down; later, when you feel confident, you can raise three up and three down. Pin the end of every working row (the ala diamond) to keep the plait from coming undone as you work around the cylinder. Be careful not to compress the towel or force wrinkles in the lining. Push the pins deep but fluff the towel from time to time. Pins stay in.

RAISING THE NEXT ALA

Sweep back all LP on the side of the cylinder facing you. Compare what you see to Figure 23 A. *Disregard* the partly worked area at the left of the drawing.

1. Lay any one of the LP to the left, across the RP.

2. Raise the first RP that this LP crosses. This is similar to Figure 23 B.

3. Lay the next LP (working toward the right) beside the first LP you laid in.

4. Lower the raised RP. This is similar to Figure 23 C.

Now use Figure 23 D through 23 I and 26 E through 26 I to help you weave the second ala. Rotate the cylinder as you progress around it, to keep a comfortable working surface and an even plait. By eye, keep your diamonds square and the angle of your working rows at 45° to the bottom and sides of the cylinder. As if by magic, a steady supply of LP will come to hand from the ala below. *Remember* to pin that last RP stroke of every working row, or you will be plaiting the same ala forever as LP escape!

When you discover only one RP understroke below the level of the ala, your situation is similar to Figure 26 G. Let 26 H and I help you finish

the ala. If the last strokes are crowded, fluff the towel and loosen the ala pins without removing them. Look for strokes that slant too much. Ease them into line and reset the pins.

Sweep back the LP and repeat for the next ala. This cylinder took me three ala of two up and one more ala of three up. Finished, it looks like Plate 140. If you have missed a stroke or two and the top is uneven, you are like everyone else who plaits her first cylinder basket. Never mind. The ribbons shine and the fusible web will hold it together. Someday when you have woven many cylinders this learner basket will show how far you have come.

Plate 140.

FINISHING THE BAG

Remove the basting and pins, except for those at the top of the cylinder. Fuse the top ala while it is still pinned to the rolled towel base. Remove the pins, then slip the plaited cylinder off the base. Follow Figure 27A – F:

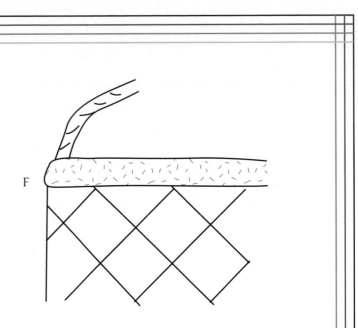

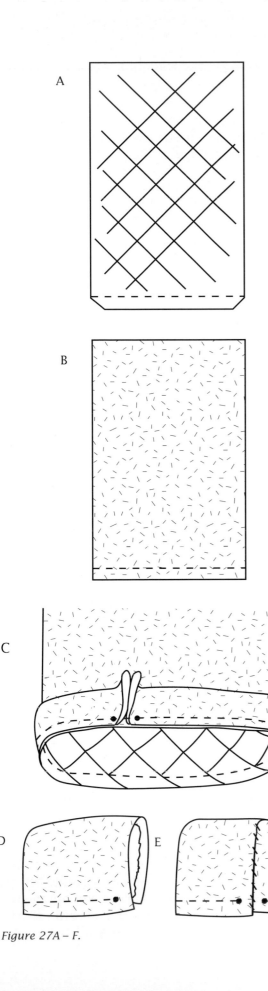

A. Trim the plaiting even with the *lining*. Flatten the cylinder anywhere, as long as the seam is not on a fold. Stitch by machine across the *end you just completed*, using ¼" seam allowance. The seam is on the outside. Trim the corners as shown.

B. Turn the bag wrong side out. Use only a blunt object to push the corners out. Tease them out with a pin from the lining side. Press the seam and the fold to flatten them. Stitch across the bag about ⅜" from the fold, enclosing the seam. Do not turn the bag right side out yet.

C. Fold the binding strip in half lengthwise, right side out. Press. Trim the open end of the cylinder ¼" beyond the points of the interlace diamonds. If any strands come unfused, pin them.

Match the raw edges of the binding to the raw edge of the lining side of the bag. Pin, leaving both ends free for overlap and joining. Stitch from the plaited ribbon side, just missing the points of the diamonds. Leave the last half inch unstitched.

D. Trim one end of the binding to ½". Fold in ¼" seam allowance.

E. Trim the other end of the binding to ½". It should just reach the start of stitching on the first end. Insert it into the opening. Hand stitch the folded seam. Hand or machine sew the last ½" of the binding-to-bag seam.

F. Turn the bag right side out. Straighten the ribbons. Fold the binding to the front. Stitch it by hand to the line of machine stitching, revealing perfect diamonds. The lining will be slightly baggy when the bag is right side out. You did not make a mistake.

Figure 27A – F.

Sew the cord of your choice to either the inside or the outside of the bag at upper corners. Tassels and bells at lower corners would add an interesting touch.

ARITHMETIC REARS ITS HEAD

How did I calculate the measurements of the lining fabric? How many ribbon strands to use? How long to cut them? As in horizontal plaiting, the number of strands, width of strands, and the size of the finished project are interdependent factors. Deciding any two determines the third. From all three we derive the lengths of strands.

Often a plaited design begins with a number of strands to suit a particular color layout. Then we decide on strand width for the best effect, and take the project size we get. Obviously we can just start a beautiful mat over uncut lining fabric, trim away the excess, and finish the bag. Learning through experimentation is fun, and we eventually discover the rules.

But with a definite objective, we juggle the three factors to suit the purpose. If size is critical, we design within that. The ribbon bag was a compromise between suitable proportion and size, and attractive strand width. (Large bags with many narrow strands allow lovely patterns but take considerable experience to plait. Small bags with wide strands end before the pattern begins.)

I divided bag size by the diagonal (D) of the strand width to estimate the number of strands (12) (Figure 28). Then I adjusted bag size to that actual commencement edge, plus expansion and seam allowance. I made the height of the bag proportional to its width.

Look back at Figure 22 and Plate 133. *The length of strands equals the diagonal measurement of a square derived from the shorter edge of the mat, plus takeup and safety allowance.* No matter where the strand starts at the commencement edge, it travels at 45° around the cylinder to reach the top. The cylinder is just a mat curved so that its sides meet. The diagonal of our 9" square is approximately 12.6". I rounded this up to 14" to allow for takeup and safety, plus seams.

CALCULATING THE COMMENCEMENT EDGE
FOR DIAGONAL PLAITING

You remember that in horizontal plaiting,

your project width (commencement edge)= (width of Vrt x number of Vrt) + expansion allowance. In *diagonal* plaiting we use a different measurement because the strands *slant*. Compare the commencement edge in Plate 133 and Figure 23 I with Figure 28.

D + D + D + D + D + D + D + D = Project width

Figure 28.

The measurement we use for calculating the space taken by a strand on the commencement edge is t*he diagonal of a square derived from the width of the strand.* The ribbon in the sample bag is ⅝" wide. The diagonal of a ⅝" square measures ⅞".

In diagonal plaiting, project width (commencement edge) = (diagonal of RP strands x number of RP strands) + expansion allowance. Why RP strands? Look at Figure 21 A and Plate 134. RP and LP occupy the same space on the commencement edge. We need to count only one of the strand sets – the one we place first in the set-up. Thus in our ribbon bag: Project width = (⅞"x 12 RP) + ½" estimated expansion = 11" commencement edge. Folded into a cylinder this mat makes a bag 5½" wide. The extra inch of lining width I allowed is seam and safety allowance, *not* part of the commencement edge.

Thus: *To calculate the length of a commencement edge,* multiply the diagonal measurement of RP x number of RP and allow for expansion.

And: *To calculate the number of RP needed for a given commencement edge,* divide that commencement edge by the diagonal measurement of RP.

Table 1 is a quick reference for the approximate ratios of common strand widths to their diagonals:

The table of larger numbers (Table 2) is a reference for the diagonal of the *mat square* (Figure 22) for calculating *lengths* of *strands*. The true ratio is 1.414 to 1. The ratio applies to inches, centimeters, or any unit of measurement. The table figures are rounded, and you can use 1.4 to 1 as a general guide, since we add expansion and generous safety allowances anyway.

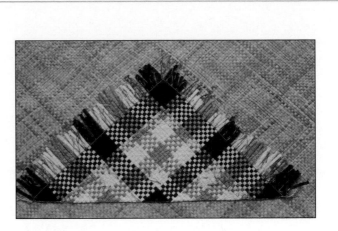

Plate 141.

Table 1

Width of Strand	Diagonal Measurement
½" (.5)	7⁄10" (.7)
5⁄8"	7⁄8"
¾"	1 1⁄10"
7⁄8"	1¼"
1"	1 4⁄10" (1.42)
1½"	2⅛" (2.13)
2"	2 8⁄10" (2.83)
2½"	3 5⁄10" (3.54)

Table 2

Width of Strand	Diagonal Measurement
10	14⅛ (14.14)
15	21¼ (21.21)
18	25½ (25.46)
24	34 (33.94)
30	42½ (42.42)
36	51 (50.91)

APPLYING YOUR NEW KNOWLEDGE

By adopting the cylinder, lining, and fusing web solutions we solved the initial problems of diagonal weave for a particular project. By knowing how to calculate different sizes, proportions, and strand lengths we open a treasure chest of ideas for the basic lined cylinder:

Strands: ribbon, ironed-over edge, glitter braid, ripped rag

Color layouts: checker, colorwash, plaid, prints through solids

Functions: sachet bag, shopping bag, sleeping bag; skirt inset, sleeves, hat crown, pillow cover, birdcage cover, garbage can cover, doll body, toy snake, wind sock. Plait! Permute! Play!

NEW ANSWERS TO OLD QUESTIONS

Let's ask for the Frog Printses' shawl and think again about those problem questions near the beginning of this chapter (Plate 141).

Compare this triangular shawl to the triangular autumn and summer hangings in Chapter 5 (Plates 69 and 70). Notice the difference in location of fringe. I began the hangings as horizontal blocks and abandoned them halfway through, on the diagonal.

The shawl takes just the opposite approach. Figures 21A and B show how it *begins* on the diagonal. This time, instead of fusing the commencement edge, I folded it over a holding cord. Its checkerwork begins with the same interlace row as shown in Plates 133 through 136, and continues with ala like the one in Figures 23 A – I, until we run out of LP and RP at the sides.

What do we do then? We abandon strand ends and call them fringe. Thus we still have neither sides nor a fourth edge to finish. I replaced the initial holding cord with pair-twined glitter braid to stabilize and decorate the commencement edge. More braid, basted, then stitched by machine, stabilizes the edges at the base of the fringe. In narrow strands, the body of diagonal checkerwork needs no stabilizing. It readjusts when laid on a flat surface after wearing.

NEW QUESTIONS FROM OLD ANSWERS

•What physical set-up makes starting, shaping, and finishing this large project easy?

•Exactly how do we lay in the strands to begin?

•The fringe is uneven. Why? What if we want it more even?

•What measurements were used for this particular shawl?

•How can we reduce or enlarge that size?

•How do we lay out color and value to obtain this balanced, plaid-like pattern?

•How was the embellishment and stabilization applied?

ADAPTING THE WEAVING BOARD

A square of flannel-backed plastic, or heavy brown paper, creased on the diagonal, makes a guide and temporary underlay. Figure 29 shows its placement and the holding cord near the edge of the board. The board lies on a table, which supports the triangular shape near half of the underlay while you place the strands. The far half of the underlay is a triangle the approximate size of the *plaited* portion of the shawl. Fringe will extend beyond the edges of the underlay.

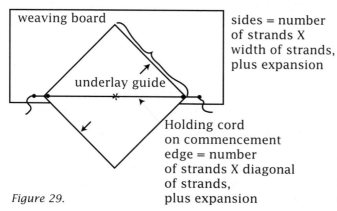

weaving board

underlay guide

sides = number of strands X width of strands, plus expansion

Holding cord on commencement edge = number of strands X diagonal of strands, plus expansion

Figure 29.

Place a pin at *, the center of the square and of the commencement edge. Also mark two arrows on your guide at centers of upper right and lower left. These help you lay strands straight. Dots at right and left represent pins holding the underlay itself.

Pins for the holding cord lie farther out, for possible expansion. The holding cord may remain in the plait permanently, in a color not easily seen between strands. Alternately, you can stabilize the edge by another method and remove the cord. The cord must be thin and firm, like string or narrow reinforcing tape, which you can dye.

SETTING UP THE STRANDS AND PLAITING

Refer to Figures 30 and 31 A – C as you lay strands on the underlay, then interlace them at the commencement edge. 31 A is a closeup view of the folded RP/LP strand in the A area of 30. In this form of Polynesian weaving, LP and RP are different ends of the same strand. Because you fold them at right angles, LP shows the reverse sides of RP strands, perfect for tube plaiting.

1. Release one end of the holding cord and lay it out of the way. Leave the pin in the board to mark the commencement edge and where to replace the cord.

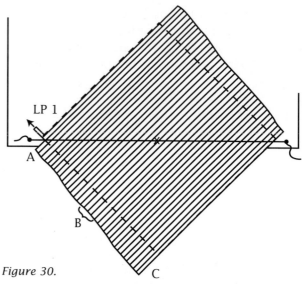

LP 1

A

B

C

Figure 30.

2. Begin at B in Figure 30, the center of the layout. On either side of the * pin lay strands running from lower left to upper right. They extend beyond the underlay for fringe. Here at the center make the fringe the same length at both ends. In Figure 30, the dashed line represents the edge of the underlay.

3. Work from the center toward sides to complete the layout. Leave a small space between strands to avoid crowding, but not too much. Make the final spacing adjustments as you plait the interlace.

Why is the fringe in the diagram uneven? Why is the fringe on the real shawl (Plate 141) even *more* uneven? Because I laid it out evenly, instead of as the diagram shows it. At the left end of the commencement edge (A) the LP you fold become fringe immediately. The RP ends of those strands weave all the way across the mat, using up their takeup allowance. Less remains for fringe. At the right end of the commencement edge (C) the situation is reversed. LP will lose length across the plait, while RP become fringe. The placement in Figure 30 evens the fringe during plaiting.

4. Replace the reinforcement cord. Pin it at the center and once more between the center and each end.

5. Convert the ends of RP to LP by folding them to the left over the holding cord. *Fold one at a time* and plait the interlace ala at the same time.

Figure 31 A – C shows how to begin. Then follow Plates 134 to 138 for the interlace ala. If the ribbon ends at the bottom of the photos confuse you, cover that part of the picture. Diagram

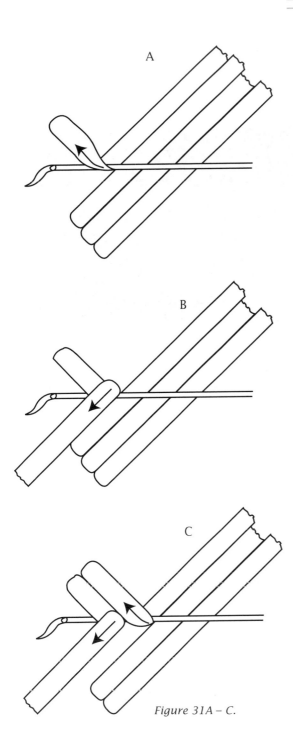

A

B

C

Figure 31A – C.

A is Plate 134. Diagram C is Plate 135.

When the interlace is complete, fold the bottom of the underlay out of your way, under the weaving board. Sit at the commencement edge.

Plait a series of ala (Figures 23 A – I) until the shawl is complete (Plate 141). Keep the plait loose enough to prevent wrinkled strands but not so loose that the center bubbles. Begin raising and lowering RP from the ala and work down the row for straighter rows. (See Plates and captions 145, 146, and 147.) Pin the edge row to the boards every two or three strands. Leave the pins in until the edge is basted or tassel tied.

CALCULATING SHAWL MEASUREMENTS

This shawl is about 42" on the commencement edge, plus fringe – long enough to reach below the waist at the front and back when draped over a shoulder. The sides measure 30", as suggested by Table 2 of mat-square to diagonal ratios. For the triangle shawl you can more easily calculate from strand *width* and triangle *side* measurement, than from strand diagonal and commencement edge. Look at Figure 30 to see how the laid-out strands equal the *sides*, and the commencement edge is the diagonal of that square.

YOU NEED:

56 tube strands of ½" *finished width*, 38" long. My original calculation for a 30" side was 60 strands, but I took out four to allow for expansion – a guess which proved accurate.

The length of strands I calculated as 28" (56 x ½") + 10% (3") takeup allowance for tube strands + 1" safety allowance + 6" fringe (3" each end). 28 + 3 + 1 + 6 = 38.

The total yardage required is 2⅓ yards of fabric at least 39" wide. To reduce a triangle (shawl) use fewer and shorter strands. To enlarge a triangle (shawl) use more and longer strands.

Table 3 contains some close estimates, including suitable allowances for fringe. Except where noted, strands are ½" tubes.

Table 3

Item	Side and Guide Square	Commencement	No. Strands	Length
Shawl	40"	57"	72	50"
Shawl	44"	63"	80	56"
Flap for front or back of yoke	10"	14"	18	18"
Ribbon Flap	5"	7"	18 of ¼" wide	14"
Ribbon Flap	2¾"	4"	19 of ⅛" wide	9"

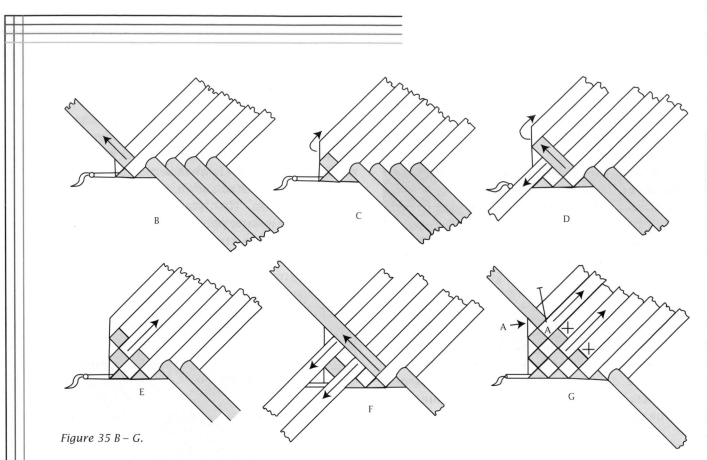

Figure 35 B – G.

B. Lay in (lower) the first LP to the right. Notice the pattern of triangles at the edges and corners of the mat.

C. Fold that LP up and to the right to become a RP. Which RP will you raise to admit the next LP?

D. Raise the understroke RP. lay in the next LP and fold *it* to become an RP.

E. Lower the RP. You now have two RP under-strokes, enough for an ala of two up and two down.

F. Raise those two RP. Lay in the next LP and leave it. We will complete the ala across the mat before returning to this left edge.

G. Lower the two RP. Pin the ala diamond to mark it. The next two RP you will raise are marked X.

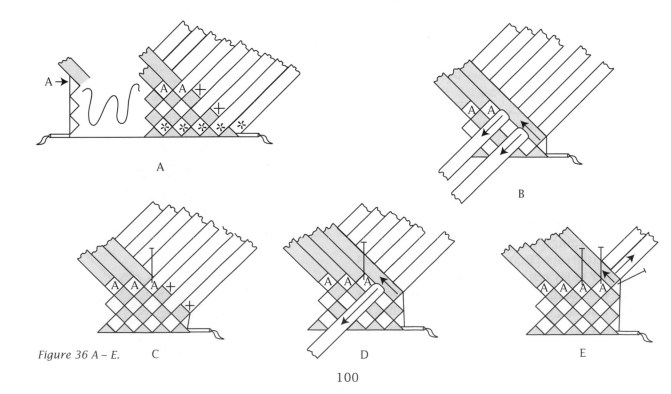

Figure 36 A – E.

Continue the ala across the mat until the last LP is laid in and that working row is closed. Use pins as needed to hold the ala.

Now follow Figure 36 A – E to fill in the ala and turn the right edge of the mat.

A. Interlace diamonds are marked * and ala diamonds A. Raise the two RP marked X.

B. With this new working row open, fold the corner (bottom) RP *under* and to the left to become an LP. Why under? Study the triangles at the corner. *Rebounding strands turn whichever way will keep the plait in checker.* In a checker-work mat started like this one, left side strands fold up, and right side strands fold under.

C. Close the row. Mark the new ala stroke with a pin. Two RP understrokes (marked X) remain below the ala. The one at the lower right will fold to become the new LP.

D. Raise the upper RP to open the row. Fold the lower RP under and to the left, into the open row.

E. Lower the RP. Mark the ala with another pin. Fold the last RP below the ala under and to the left. This forms the last half-diamond at the right-hand end of the ala. Pin it. This end should be the same distance from the commencement edge as the starting end of the ala. If the ala drops or rises, the angle of RP 1 has wandered off the true diagonal.

Return to the left edge of the mat. Sweep back the LP and repeat the steps of Figures 35 and 36 as many times as needed for your project. When you feel confident, raise larger ala.

Pin every fourth or fifth ala diamond as you go. If, the pins on the lower ala catch on strands, remove them. Pin the mat *sides* about every third triangle.

STABILIZING THE EDGES

Pair-twined braid or a holding cord with blanket stitch secures the edges. You could work with a holding cord along both sides from the initial set-up. I find it easier to thread one through with a blunt (tapestry) needle after finishing the mat. I tie more cord to the existing one, hiding the knot between layers. I do this before removing edge pins and make sure to pull it snug. I carry it around the fourth edge as well and catch it in the fourth edge finish.

Finish the fourth side with braid or a straight strip of folded fabric, stitched at the base of the fringe, through the last ala. The "Weaver Wizards" skirt has tied tassels on sides and fringe edge, with no holding cord on those sides. They decorate as well as stabilize.

A WORD ABOUT THE NATURE OF DIAGONAL MATS

Because they are bias weave, diagonal mats do not hang well on walls. They drape. They lie on beds and floors. They cling to the human body. The "Sunset of the Weaver Wizards" skirt is a 56-strand mat, the same as the shawl, but extended into a fringed rectangle. Its holding cord gathers the waist as it wraps and hooks around a very slim model. It looks better on her than on the wall.

HOW LONG IS A STRAND? DO A DOUBLETAKE

For square or rectangular mats, compute from diagonal measurements. Figure the commencement edge from strand diagonals (Figure 28). Obviously all sides of a square mat measure the same as the commencement edge.

The diagonal measurement of a square equals one side multiplied by 1.414 (Table 2 and Figure 22). In "Arithmetic Rears Its Head" you learned to make strands this long, plus suitable takeup, safety, and edge finishing allowances for the strand type. Look again at Figures 33 and 34. Because LP and RP are the same strand, *double* this measurement. No matter what its actual course through the square, the length of its journey remains the same. Two sample calculations follow.

1. A mat 20" square measures 20" x 1.414 (28½") on the diagonal, plus 10% takeup for tube strands (3") plus 1" safety allowance, plus 4" minimum for finishing the fourth edge with or without fringe. This totals 36½". Double this for the combined RP/LP strand (73"). You can turn a strand this length through an opening in its side.

2. A mat 40" square takes almost twice as much. 40" x 1.414 (57") plus 10% (6") plus 1", plus 4" totals 68". Doubled this equals 136". For strands this length you have two options:

•Hand-join shorter strands, keeping the join away from the exact center (commencement edge).

•Go back to the ribbon handbag layout, with separate LP and RP sets. Add fringe at the commencement edge as well.

Chapter Nine
THINKING YOUR WAY OUT OF A CORNER

CORNER-START DIAGONAL MATS

In the islands, holding cords support waistbands of dancing skirts that may or may not begin with an ala of checkerwork before the long fringes fall free. True mats, on the other hand, commence with interlaced tag sets (fine mats) or they commence at the lower left-hand corner with LP/RP strands like you used for the rag rug. These corner-start mats need no holding cord in firm pandanus and the double-layer construction method used for floor mats.

For our rectangular diagonal weave mats in cloth, we can adapt this quick corner start to single-layer weave, eliminating both holding cord and interlace. What do we have to do?

•Turn mat edges carefully, using an underlay guide or drawn lines.

•Use more pins on the commencement edge to compensate for no cord.

•Plan the layout in advance instead of cruising from the center.

Is it worth it? Are there other advantages than a simple start? Since we already use the underlay for straight edges, the extra pins are the main drawback. The advantage is having an established ala as a firm weaving base, right from the start.

PRE-PLANNING A PROJECT

Before working in cloth, study this chapter with a mat in mind of 20 combined LP/RP strands. Think of tube strands of one inch finished width in a layout of values in groups of five. As you read, practice on a colored paper mat. Half-inch strips will give you a ¼ size model. Working from a paper model to a fabric product will help you to appreciate the usefulness of this design approach.

Figure 37 shows a convenient physical setup for corner-start on a large scale. The weaving board can slide away from you at the start of early ala, when swept-back LP are long and need a place to lie. As the mat deepens, pull the board toward you and place the pincushion on it

At the left a rack, or a pole between chair backs, holds strands with pins marking their centers, sorted into color sets. A large pin for

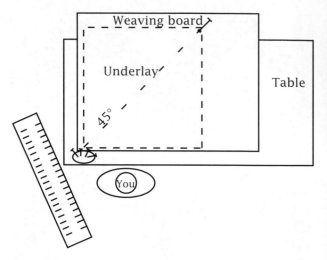

Figure 37.

sighting the true diagonal is at the upper right. When you lay in the first doubled strand (Figure 38 A) its extended ends straddle that pin. As you lay in additional strands, they parallel the first two, but you can pin them into loose bobbins, as we did for "Rag Rug Rumble." Let them out as you need the length.

DESIGNING FROM THE CORNER

We think differently from the corner than from the center of the commencement edge. The center focuses attention on the diamond path of center strands. (See Figure 33.) This tempts us to balance left and right, with a solid block at dead center where corner diagonals cross.

Designing from the corner focuses attention on the diagonal path of the first strands laid in. Is it a beam of light? A shadow? A ray of pure color? Will an identical twin cross it from the other corner, forming an X, or will the balance of this mat become more complex?

In Plate 150 three sample cloth strip mats demonstrate three layout strategies for your paper models using value groups of five strands. These effects work for corner start and for center start alike. They are like quilt blocks of the same pattern made up in different values.

In mat A we use only three values, repeating one from both corners. This makes a plain cen-

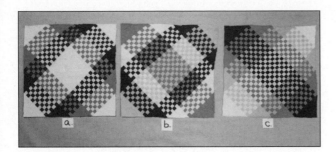

Plate 150.

tral area and four corner triangles the same. However, we have laid aside the temptation to balance exactly. Values change at the center of the commencement edge. This forces the high-contrast rectangular checkerboards to exchange places around the center with checkerboards of moderate contrast.

In mat B we shift two different medium values to the corners. The center area becomes a low-contrast checkerboard. Maximum contrast checkers scatter to the four edges, and the offset light and dark strands skew the balance.

Mat C employs our old light-to-dark shading strategy. Whether the ray of light or the shadow dominates depends partly on how light or dark the two medium values are. Turning the mat on its side may change our perception as well.

If the offset balance of A and B disturb you, turn all the mats on point – formal balance again. You'll notice that my fused cloth mats are not quite straight. This happens in most cloth mats, like the wandering strands of real pandanus mats. This is the nature of the medium. You can minimize it or emphasize it to suit your purpose.

Look at the diagonal paths of corner strands in all the mats. Why are they so wide when we used only five strands in each value group? Look at the rag rug in Plate 148. The three dark strands I laid in at each corner are stronger than the five at the center of the commencement edge. Look again at Figure 33 and the paths of strands that originate at the corners. A strand in the corner is worth two at the edge.

When planning layouts, remember that every strand in the corner value group increases the ray by two. If you don't want that wide effect, reduce the corner value group. Constructing a corner will make this clear.

BUILDING FROM THE CORNER

Select one of the layout strategies for a paper strip exercise. Follow Figures 38, 39, 40, and 42 As your strands run out, replace them by overlapping.

The commencement corner is our old stand-by, the arrowhead turn, placed at a 45° angle as the base of two RP. To build the first ala and the commencement edge at the same time, we lay in LP for each new working row, then convert them to RP.

A. At the lower-left corner of your underlay place an arrowhead, folded as shown. Pin the corner at the dot. Note that the emerging understroke comes from the left edge of the mat-to-be. The overstroke comes from the commencement edge. If you reverse these folds, you must reverse all other edge folds to keep those edge triangles. I fold this way because everyone I learned from starts floormats this way. The commencement edge folds easily.

B. Raise the RP understroke.

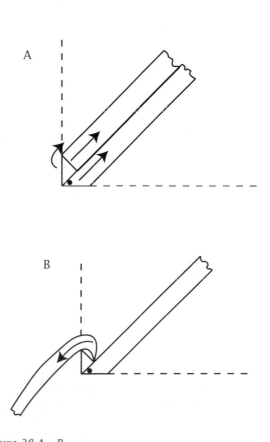

Figure 38 A – B.

105

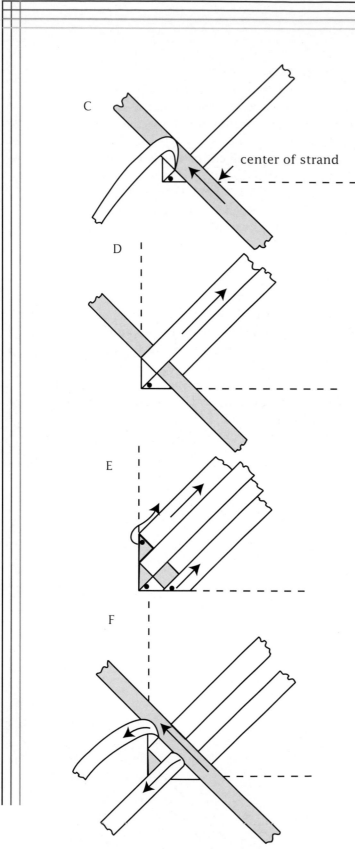

center of strand

Figure 38 C – I.

C. Lay in a new strand with its center at the commencement edge. This is the LP of the first working row.

D. Lower the raised RP. What do you do with

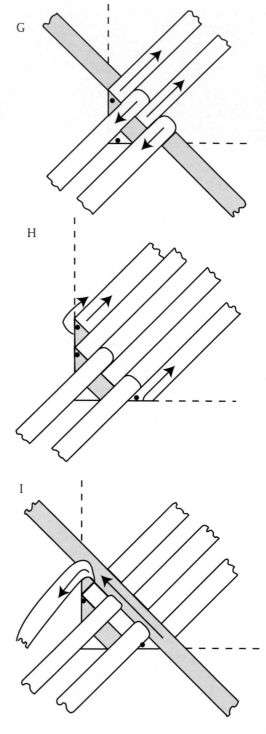

the ends of the LP?

E. Convert them to RP. Fold the commencement edge end upward and to the right, like the corner strand. Fold the left end under and to the right, like that end of the corner strand. Pin them. The checkerwork is established. Which RP do we raise next?

F. The two understrokes. Lay in the next strand, center at the commencement edge.

G. Close that row as you open the next. Coordinate your hands.

H. Then fold the commencement and left edges. Pin. You now have six RP, two of them raised for the next working row.

I. The RP at the left edge is always an understroke after you fold it. Lift that strand to complete the checker sequence. Lay in the next strand.

Repeat this sequence – new strand in, row closed and next row open, ends folded, left edge RP lifted, new strand in – until you have an ala of five up (Figure 39A). Pin each edge fold.

A. Five up is a reasonable depth. Keep the 45° angle by sighting the corner strands on the pin occasionally. Lay in a new strand as usual.

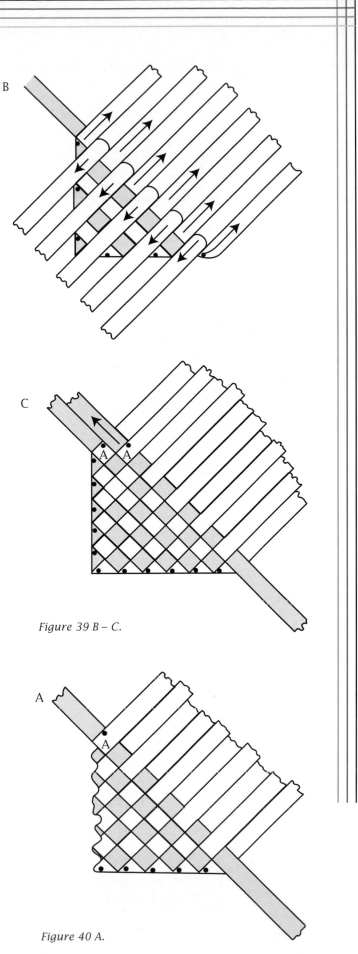

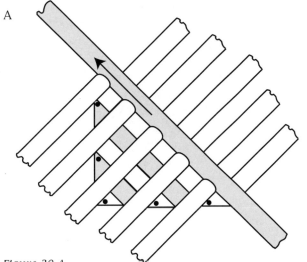

Figure 39 A.

B. Close that row and open the next. You now have five up without folding the LP at the left edge. Let it protrude from the mat. Fold the commencement edge end only.

C. Lay in a new strand. Close the row and find the ala diamonds, which are always RP, remember. Mark them with pins.

Continue across the mat with this ala of five up and five down until you have laid in the last strand and closed that row. (See Figure 40 A.) This sequence of working is: new strand in, row closed and next row open, commencement edge folded, new strand in.

A. Folding the corner and building the right-hand edge of the mat is similar to Figures 36 A – E, except for folding the strands under or upward. Which fold produces triangles at the edges and corners? Use that fold.

Figure 39 B – C.

Figure 40 A.

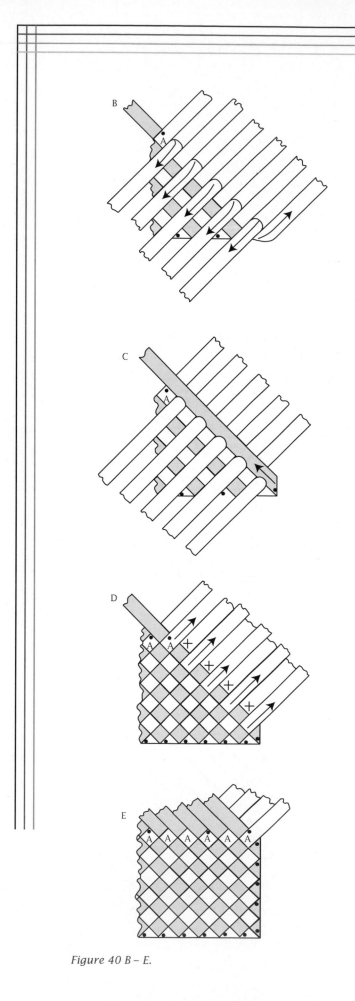

Figure 40 B – E.

Follow me through 40 B – D, then fill in the ala to 40 E on your own.

B. At the commencement edge fold the new strand up and to the right. Raise all under-strokes below the ala to open the row, as usual. What will you lay into that row?

C. Turn the last RP back into an LP. Fold it upward to form two corner triangles, and left into the row. Pin the corner.

D. Close the row. Mark the ala with a pin. How many understrokes remain below the ala? They are marked X.

Now your sequence of working is: LP folded and laid in, row closed, next row open, right-hand mat edge turned as LP is folded and laid in. You will find that LP fold upward at the right edge, just as strands folded upward at the commencement edge. These two edges fold the same way in any diagonal mat. Left and finishing edges both fold opposite to the commencement edge.

E. The right-hand edge should look like this, completed up to the ala.

Sweep all loose LP back for the next ala. Return to the left edge of the mat and raise a new ala. Figures 38 and 39 will help, but instead of new strands you lay the established LP into the working rows.

A HINT ABOUT PINNING

Pins at the left and right edges keep you from pulling edge folds out of place as you work the strand connected to them. As the weaving moves away from that fold, remove some of the pins, perhaps three out of four. Ala need only be pinned on every third or fourth diamond, and pins from lower ala can be removed. Avoid wearing knit or trailing sleeves!

THE FINAL EDGE AT LAST

Raise as many ala as needed to complete the square pattern. Fringe, if any, protrudes beyond the last ala.

For a zigzag hand-appliquéd fourth edge like Lanu Lalanga (Plate 151) stop at the end of the pattern. Stabilize the three finished edges while the mat is on the board. Then remove pins from the fourth edge, and use each one to pin the cloth layers of the final ala diamonds together. Remove the mat from the board.

A. Cut off each strand ½" beyond the edge of the last strand it crosses.

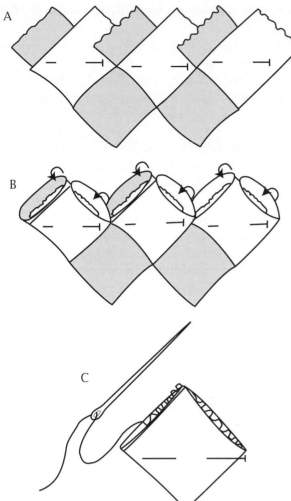

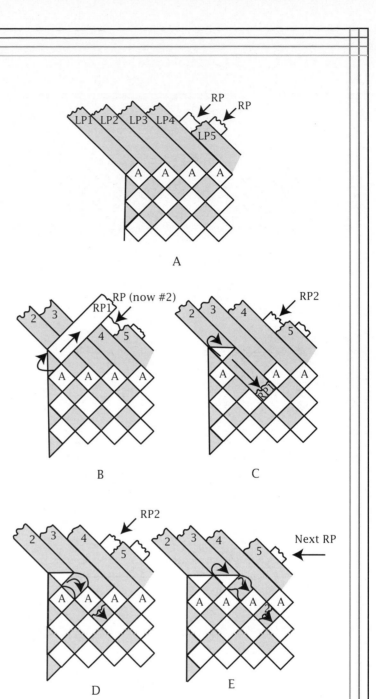

Figure 41 A – C.

Figure 42 A – E.

B. Fold raw edges to the inside of each tube, with the fold even with the edge of the strand crossed.

C. Ladderstitch the tube ends closed. At the same time take a few stitches through the fold of the strand crossed, securing all layers.

This hand-stitched finish is good for fabric tubes. For paper or ribbon mats, the classic pandanus mat turndown makes an edge of triangles. However, it tends to widen the top edge of the mat. You may find this edge distortion acceptable in rag rugs and useful in art pieces. With turned-down ends left dangling on the face of the mat, it has potential as embellishment.

Figures 42 A – K show a simplified version. Polynesian weavers fold and plait the LP ends into the final ala. Instead, we will tuck them into place after finishing the ala.

A. After completing the last ala leave LP lying across RP. Return to the left-hand edge.

B. Fold LP 1 under and to the right, as usual. Call it RP 1 now.

C. Fold RP 1 under and downward toward the right. You have turned the third corner of the mat. The end of RP 1 lies on top of LP 2.

D. Slip the end of RP 1 under the top RP strokes that cross LP 2. Take them under two if length permits. Needlenose pliers can help.

Leave LP 2 extending from the back of the mat. Locate the first of the remaining RP (RP 2) which lies behind LP 3 and 4.

E. Bring RP 2 out from behind all LP. Fold it under and downward to the right, on top of LP 3.

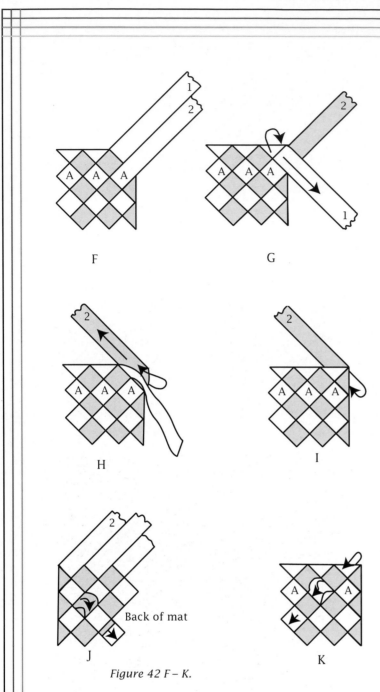

F   G

H   I

J   Back of mat

K

Figure 42 F – K.

Insert its end under RP overstrokes, as before. Continue turning RP in this manner, across the mat, forming edge triangles above the ala. Stop when only two RP remain.

F. These remaining RP will form the fourth corner of the mat. (From here on I have not drawn the LP extending from the back of the mat, except in Figure J.)

G. Fold RP 1 under and downward to the right, in front of RP 2.

H. Fold RP 2 upward and to the left, behind the folded strand 1. This is consistent with other right-hand edge folds. In the diagram strand 1 is rolled up for you to see RP 2 folded underneath, now LP.

I. Fold strand 1 under, to the back of the mat.

J. On the back, lead strand 1 downward to the right to secure it.

K. On the front, fold the last LP over the top of the corner. Lead it downward to the left, through as many overstrokes as it reaches.

OPTIONS FOR STABILIZING THE FOURTH-EDGE TURNDOWN

•For paper: Glue overlaps and cut off strand ends on front and back.

•For ribbon or frayed-edge strands: Fuse or fabric-glue overlaps and cut off strand ends. Or tie tassels through overlaps and cut off strand ends. Or fold all LP as well as RP to the front of the mat. Lead them under one overstroke and let them fall free. Tie tassels to secure. Trim and fray-proof points on ribbons and pull loose threads to fray raw-edge strands.

•For a concealed finish on tubes and rag rugs, pin the overlaps and cut off ends. Hand appliqué overstrokes on one side to keep strand ends from pulling out, and on their other sides to hide raw ends.

ARITHMETIC AGAIN

Everything you need to know you learned in Chapter 8, but some hints will help you apply it to new situations like rectangular mats.

The bigger the mat, the more safety allowance you need. Not just extra length of strands, but their tendency to wander off course increases the chance of running out.

Wider strands need more turndown allowance. The suggested 4" allowance works well for ½" strands, but 1" strands may run out before completing the lead-away at corners.

In pandanus, paper, and rag rugs, adding strands as they run out means only planning steps 1 and 3 below need to be done. The arithmetic takes care of itself. For your tube strand mat, do all the steps.

1. Plan your layout pattern of value and color, how many strands and how wide.

2. From these, calculate the length of the commencement edge, allowing for expansion.

3. Decide whether your mat will be square (closed pattern) or rectangular (repeating some or all of the pattern).

4. Sketch this shape with the measurements of its edges (Figure 43). Figure the length of the

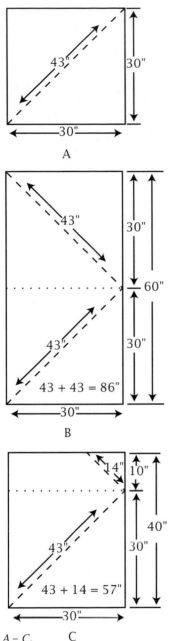

A

B

C

Figure 43 A – C.

result, you need the challenge of awkward questions.

•What if you use hand-dyed strands that change color radically over their lengths? Does it matter which end of a strand you lay to the left?

•What if you use a new color or shade for every strand you lay in, graduating them along the commencement edge?

•What if you piece related prints and solids into a sheet (using very short stitches) and cut strands across the pieced sheet? Use strands from two or more such sheets as "value sets" in your layout pattern.

Plate 151. "Lanu Lalanga" (Color Woven), 46" x 51" ©1993 Shari Cole. A diagonal, corner start mat of 22 tube strands (layout groups of 5, 6, 6, and 5 strands). Color changes are planned and sometimes sudden, dye-painted for the purpose. The commencement edge is at the top of the picture. As in mat C of Figure 43, corner strands complete one diagonal crossing and rebound for a partial repeat. Even considering the color changes within strands, unexpected patterns have emerged. Why?

diagonal course of the first corner strand. Mat A is one pattern repeat, mat B adds another repeat in mirror image. Mat C repeats one third of the pattern, mirrored.

5. Calculate the length of strands from this measurement, plus allowances, and double it. The figures in the diagram are for hypothetical mats. Substitute your own measurements. Use Chapter 8 for reference.

FLYING TIME – COLOR WOVEN

Now that you know where every strand falls in a diagonal mat, and what checkerboards will

Chapter Ten
A NEW SLANT ON TWILL

TWILL FIGURES IN DIAGONAL MATS

Were you tempted to try twill on your corner start mat? Those tidy checkerboards beg for excitement. The centers of mats B and C (Plate 150) cry out for twill medallions to give them purpose.

In Lanu Lalanga (Plate 151) did you see patterns of skipped strands among the confusion of color? One ala of yellow and turquoise RP skipping over two LP marches across the lower third of the mat. Above, interlaced with these, peach, purple, and turquoise LP march resolutely in the opposite direction, skipping over two RP. Lost in the colors above, a more complicated twill ala divides the top third of the mat from the center.

Study the meeting of pale yellow and turquoise in the lower right-hand corner of the mat. A crossed box figure of turquoise strands skipping over two and over three yellow strands is repeated three times at the left and in the center in varied color combinations. Can you find them?

Look at the *horizontal* mats in Plate 113. This box figure appears at the lower right on the smaller mat, and twice on the left side of the larger mat. Tilt the page to place these blocks on point and compare the figures.

Diagonal twill takes mental gymnastics until you do so much of it that your hands know the steps by themselves. We will make a start here. The journey is up to you. As in horizontal twill, simple figures are the most useful for direct work with cloth. If instead you are electrified by the idea of piecing quilts designed by plaiting paper, your journey will be long and interesting.

In diagonal plaiting we use twill in the same three ways as in horizontal plaiting:

•as medallions to dominate a ground checkerwork

•as figures scattered informally across checkerwork

•as all over repeat patterns

In *horizontal* weave we build up the twill pattern one horizontal working row at a time, across the entire mat. To understand the construction of twill figures in a diagonal mat, view them horizontally. Tilt the mat onto its lower left-hand corner so you see *right pointers as verticals,* the working strands of the weave. Left pointers function as horizontals, the strands laid into open working rows.

In *diagonal* weave we also build up twill pattern one working row at a time. But because we work with ala of limited depth, we can't work the whole row at once. What can you do?

•Start with small twill figures that fit into one ala.

•Work the figures within one value group, more easily kept track of.

•Learn simple skip patterns to repeat along the ala – over two, over two, over two.

•Realize that you can continue a figure above the ala to finish it. Mark the area with pins and return to the ala. The pins will remind you on the next ala that your count is temporarily disturbed. The ala system is a *convenience,* not an edict.

•Learn to keep track of a partly completed figure from one ala to the next. Weave it one ala at a time as you come to it.

AN EXPERIMENT WITH OLD IDEAS
IN NEW COMBINATIONS

Let's make a small quilt top mat to layer with batting and backing. Let's go out on a limb and combine some permutations we haven't tried together yet:

Strand type – ironed-over edge

Set – diagonal, with LP and RP as separate strands, ribbon bag set up

Twill – random figures in checkerwork ground

Value Layout – RP in prints, as single strands washing from lights to dark mediums; LP in solids, value groups progressing from very light to medium.

We have an immediate problem. When you fold ironed-over edge strands at the edge of a mat, the wrong side comes to the surface. What do we have to do?

•Fuse the commencement edge as for the ribbon bag in Chapter 8.

•Carry LP and RP off left and right edges. Cut them off outside the edge *line.* Reinsert the rest of the strand, right side up, in the position it would normally occupy. LP ends become new RP. RP ends become new LP.

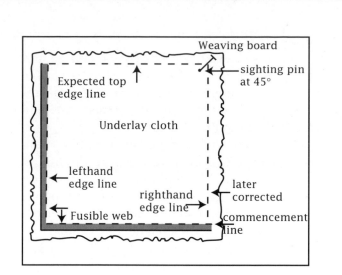

Figure 45.

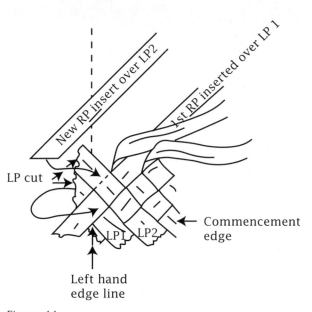

Figure 44.

Other questions remain. How can we secure the other three edges, and the unstable bias body of the mat in order to lift it and lay it on batting and backing? Here's what I did.

I cut a piece of flimsy waste cloth larger than the expected size of the mat. This was the underlay with extra margin for handling.

I drew some guidelines on it for all four sides, then placed the commencement and left edges on these two lines. After plaiting the interlace I redrew the right-hand edge line where the expansion of the commencement edge actually placed it. See Figure 45.

Before laying out the strands I applied a strip of fusible web to the *outside* of the commencement and left edge lines. After correcting the right edge line, I applied web to its outside. Why outside? The web secures only the strand ends, not the plait.

When the plaiting was finished, instead of fusing the top, I basted along the top points of the ala diamonds, marking the stitching line for the border at the same time.

The underlay stabilizes the bias body. I basted a widely spaced *horizontal/vertical grid*, similar to basting the blocks in Chapter 6.

PROCEDURE: TECHNICAL NOTES FOR STARTING TOGETHER, THEN FOLLOWING YOUR OWN PATH

For my permutation quilt (Plates 152, 153, 94) I chose a familiar layout and measurements, and a small format to simplify working with new variables.

Measurements: 20 RP and 20 LP in *finished* width of 1" strands

Diagonal of 1" strand = 1.41"

20 strands x 1.41" = 28½" + estimated expansion for ironed over edge strands 1½" = commencement edge 30" minimum

Sides therefore 30" minimum as well.

Strand length: Diagonal of the square about 42".

42" + 8% takeup allowance (3") + safety 1" + seam allowances, finish and start 2" + extra for cut and restart at side 2" = 50" strands

Hints for strands: Machine piece the 50" length before you iron the edges. Keep strands partly rolled during weaving to prevent the edges from uncurling. Unroll RP 1 to sight on the pin.

Physical set-up: Lay out as for the ribbon bag, *except* pin instead of fuse. Do not fuse the commencement edge until you finish the interlace ala and make any adjustments to spacing of strands.

Value layout: RP: 20 low-contrast prints in varied scale, shaded left to right, light to dark medium; LP: solid and subtle textures: 3 very light, 7 light, 7 light medium, 3 medium

The groups of same-fabric LP impose some order on a fragmented scatter of prints and allow twill figures worked in the same fabric.

Surprises await. We have separated LP and RP into prints and solids. As LP and RP exchange positions, so do prints and solids. Your own fabric choice will determine the contrast level and mood of your quilt.

Work first with a paper model as we walk through some twill figures. For paper "prints" of darkening values, scribble or rubber stamp on tinted paper, shading the density of the marks. Cut strands from different densities. Begin the mat with an interlace ala (Plates 133 – 138).

Raise a second ala, building up the left edge. Figures 44 and 35 A – G will help you. Plate 152 shows my fabric mat. Establish an ala of three up, to give you six RP to work through value groups of six and seven LP. Three up and three down places your working row in the group of seven light LP. Figure 46 shows your position.

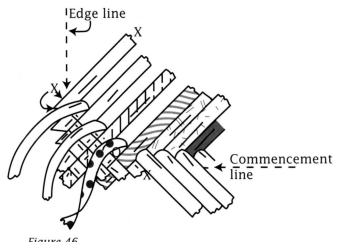

Figure 46.

You have cut and reinserted the first LP as an RP (those strands marked X). The second light LP is ready to lay into the open row. You have one completed row of checkerwork in the light LP group (under the three raised RP). Since every twill figure begins with a single overstroke, count the RP marked 0 as the first movement, the center bottom, of a figure.

Let's do the crossed box. Figure 47 compares its formation in horizontal and diagonal twill. In both methods, the working strands (light) are left down, and the laid strands (dark) skip over.

In *horizontal* twill the figure grows from a single overstroke at its center bottom. Addition-

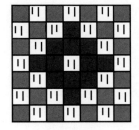 

Horizontal	Diagonal
Vrt. Light	RP Light
Hrz. Dark	LP Dark

Figure 47.

al working rows of the figure sit directly above one another, from bottom to top. The figure's center occupies the same position in each working row, and uses the same vertical strand.

In *diagonal* twill, we center the figure at the *bottom* (right-hand end) of the *working row* (marked 0 in Figure 46). Working rows are *offset* as you proceed along the ala. The center strand of the figure changes relative position in each successive working row. The box figure just fits into an ala of three up and three down.

Follow Figure 48 A – F to complete this figure. Raw edges on the backs of cloth strands are not shown in the drawings. Since you are working with light prints and solids, I have not shaded the LP to match Figure 47. Instead I have indicated where the print RP start in this layout.

A. The overstroke marked 0 is in working row 1 of the figure. In working row 2 the LP must skip over three RP. The RP on either side of stroke 0 are already down. (See Figure 46.) Lower the center RP as well. Checker the rest of the row up to the ala.

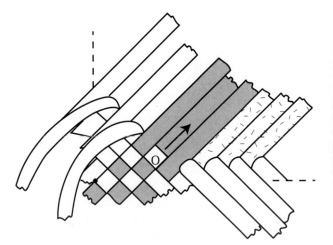

Figure 48 A.

114

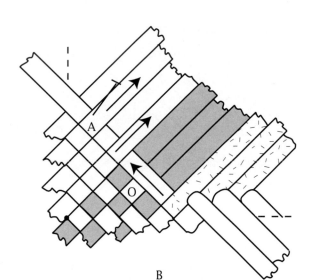

B

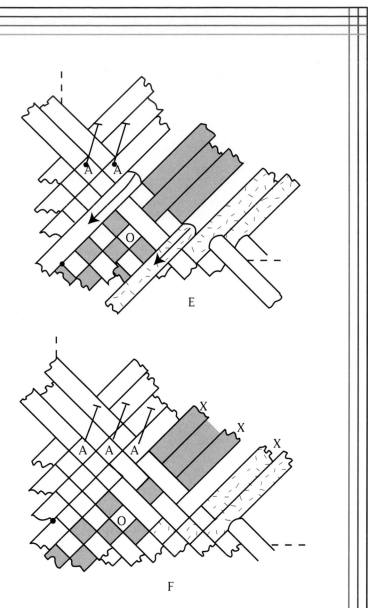

E

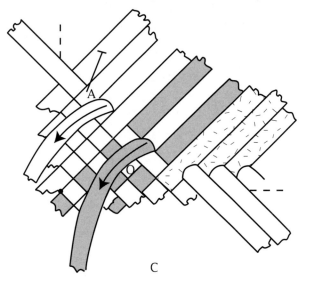

C

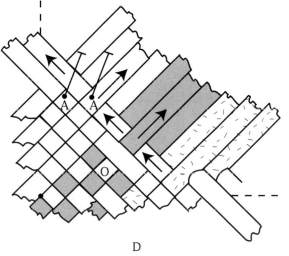

D

F

Figure 48 B – F.

B. Lay in the LP for row 2. Lower raised RP to see that row. Pin the ala diamond – the top stroke you just lowered. Compare this to the diagonal figure in Figure 47.

In working row 3 the LP must pass over two, under one, over two, under one, and out above the ala. Which RP will you raise?

C. Raise the RP at the center of the figure, plus the one that will form the ala diamond.

D. Lay in the next LP. Lower all RP to see working row 3 completed. Pin the ala. This is the central working row of the figure.

In row 4 the LP must skip over three RP at the center of the figure. Which three will you leave down? Which RP will you raise to finish the row in checker?

E. Leave these three down. Raise RP to the right and to the left, to hem in the long twill stroke. This fills the row.

F. Lay in the LP. Lower all RP to see row 4 completed. It is like row 2, except that the checkerwork is now at the bottom (right-hand side) of the row. Pin the ala.

To complete the figure, return to checker by raising RP marked X.

Work another row or two in checker, then try another figure, perhaps a series of the X cross. Plate 152 shows the figures I wove using these diagrams.

Near the right-hand edge, return to checker. If you need help with the edge, refer to Figure 36 A – E. Cut RP outside the edge and reinsert them as LP. Keep the points of edge diamonds on the right edge line.

Return to the left edge and raise another ala of two RP up. Let's make a streak of twill across the mat. Again use the solid LP for overstrokes. Figure 49 A shows your starting position.

A. Pin the new ala. The easiest twill repeat is over three, over three, over three. You enter this pattern directly from checker with no intermediate steps. Which group of three RP will you leave down? Which RP will you raise for the top stroke of the ala?

B. Leave down three RP closest to the first ala. Raise the understroke immediately above those three to secure the long LP overstroke. Lay in the next LP.

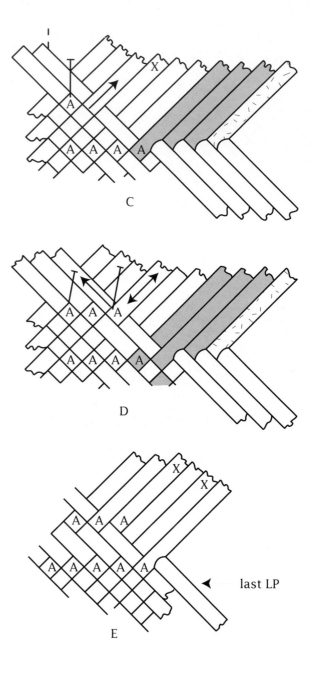

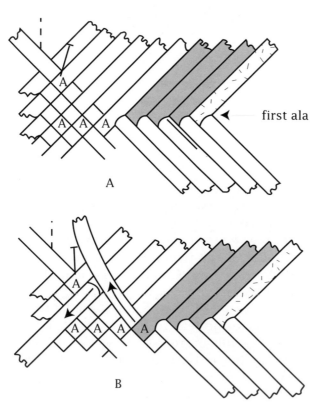

Figure 49 A – E.

To plait repeat twill we usually work one LP overstroke and one RP overstroke for each working row. The order of working is: RP raised, LP down, RP down.

The rhythm of the hands is: left hand scoops while the right hand holds. Right hand (LP) down. Left hand (RP) down. This means the left hand scoops up the RP while the right hand steadies the row. The right hand lays in the next LP, and the left hand lowers the RP it just raised. Then it moves on to the next working row. Step B shows "RP raised" and "LP down."

C. Complete the sequence with "RP down." X marks the next RP.

D. Repeat the order of working on the next row. Leaving three RP down at the bottom of the row, raise the next RP. Lay in the LP. Lower the RP. In each working row the twill stroke is offset by one strand as it follows the line of the first ala.

E. Continue across the mat as far as you like. Before you reach the right edge, return to checker. Lift two RP understrokes, marked X, instead of one. Fill in the edge with checkerwork.

Plate 152. Left and commencement edges of the permutation quilt in progress. The black strip follows the outside points of the edge diamonds placed exactly on the drawn lines of the underlay. Points are on the stitching lines for border or binding.

Because we set up the commencement edge as for the ribbon bag, strands cut and reinserted at the left edge go over the old LP ends. Strands we cut and reinsert at the right edge go under the old RP ends.

Return to the left edge. Decide which twill figures to include in the next ala. An ala of four up and four down accommodates the figure in Plate 109 and the "butterfly" in Figures 18 A – G.

Continue adding ala until you reach the top edge. The drawn line is a guide only. The top ala may fall above or below it, but must be straight to produce a straight quilt.

You have reached the third corner (upper left) when the last solid color LP you placed at the right-hand end of the commencement edge reaches the upper left-hand edge of the mat. This completes the pattern with a diagonal line across the mat center.

With tube strands you would fold the corner here. Instead cut the strand off and place it as a

new RP. It passes over only *one* LP, the one you cut it from. In Plate 153 the white push pin anchors this RP at the corner. The white paper strip follows the line of pins along the left edge and the top ala, just begun. This is the stitching line for the binding or border. Note the edge triangles.

Plate 153. Left and top edges of the permutation quilt in progress. The white strip follows the outside points of the edge and ala diamonds. Compare this to Plate 152.

Fuse the sides of your cloth mat. Baste the top edge. Mark and trim a line ½" outside the points of the edge diamonds, for seam allowance. Baste lightly in a grid for handling. Add the border if there is to be one. Rotate the quilt top in all directions and decide which way is up.

If you want trails of glitter braid or ribbon for embellishment, apply them now. You might weave them over and under strands, like the ribbons in "Starry Eyed Down the Garden Path." Sew the embellishment by hand or machine.

Layer the top, batting, and backing. Baste, and quilt by hand or machine. I hand quilt/appliqué large twill figures and twill rows. There are too many stops and starts for efficient machine quilting. Often I add machine meander quilting in other areas of the quilt. Add lines of beads and other embellishments by hand.

DIVERGING PATHS: LEFT AND RIGHT GO THEIR OWN WAYS

When we wove a shawl, rambled through a rug, and thought from a corner, we worked with single strands that included both RP and LP. Each strand wove a rectangular course, creating plaid-like patterns.

This time we separated RP and LP into prints and solids. Prints went right and rebounded from the right-hand edge. Solids went left and rebounded from that edge. Figure 50 A shows the four triangular areas that developed from this layout plan.

Over this print/solid layout we superimposed a value distribution layout. Figure 50 B shows the paths of four sample strands and the areas of high and low contrast created by their intersections. Note in Plate 94 the actual path of yellow solid strands, which skews the fall of light.

Twill rows and figures that cross value boundaries erase the hard lines between areas. The effect is complex. Keeping value contrast relatively low makes it subtle.

PLAYING A NEW ANGLE

Let's go off on a tangent. We mentioned strands crossing at angles other than 90° (Plate 15). When we ask for a new angle, we ask many questions:

What happens to the shapes we see where left and right strands cross?

How would a steep set change twill figures?

How will we set up the commencement edge?

How do measurements of commencement edge and strand length change?

How can we keep the angle consistent and diamonds uniform?

How will steep angle affect mat shape?

If bias mats distort easily, are these neither-bias-nor-straight mats worse?

Find out what happens to checkerwork and to twill figures by plaiting a series of paper mats set at different angles. Simplify the layout to start with – RP light, LP dark. Move on to cloth mats.

It may surprise you that the mat remains rectangular, but one layout pattern repeat is no longer square. (Figures 51 and 52). When you fold a strand at equal angles to the edge, the edge remains straight. However, a shallow strand angle at the commencement edge becomes a steep angle as it rebounds from the sides. Keep LP parallel and RP parallel, and the angles will take care of themselves.

Once edges are stabilized, these not-quite-bias mats behave much like bias mats. They may not drape as well. You can plait them over an underlay, as for our bias permutations quilt.

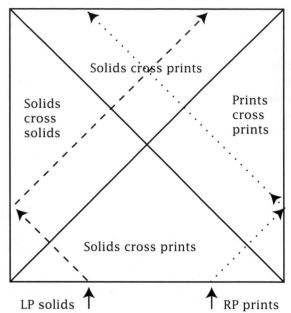

A. Print/Solid distribution

Solids cross prints

Solids cross solids

Prints cross prints

Solids cross prints

LP solids ↑   ↑ RP prints

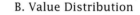

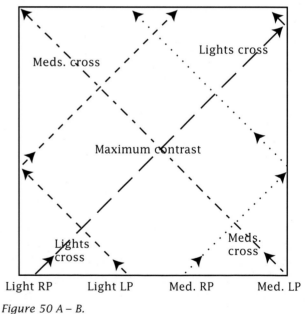

B. Value Distribution

Meds. cross

Lights cross

Maximum contrast

Lights cross

Meds. cross

Light RP   Light LP   Med. RP   Med. LP

Figure 50 A – B.

Trace the course of strands through these three mats. Single pattern repeats A and B are rectangles determined by the set-up angle. The sighting pin in the upper right-hand corner of the mat is for the lower left-hand corner strand. Place a second pin halfway up the right side of the mat. Sight the center strand of the layout on that.

If the commencement edge expands farther than expected, those strands will still pass the sighting pins at the correct angle, on their way to the right-hand edge. They meet the edge higher up. As in Figure 52 C, relocate pins to the true corner, bottom center, and halfway point after establishing the commencement edge. The diagram supposes a corner start. For a center layout start, the bottom center pin need not move. Add corresponding pins at top left and center left to sight in both directions.

Mat D demonstrates locating pins for mats with more than one pattern repeat.

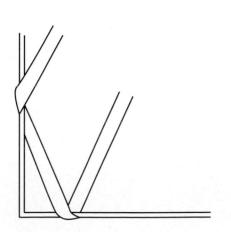

Figure 51 A – C.

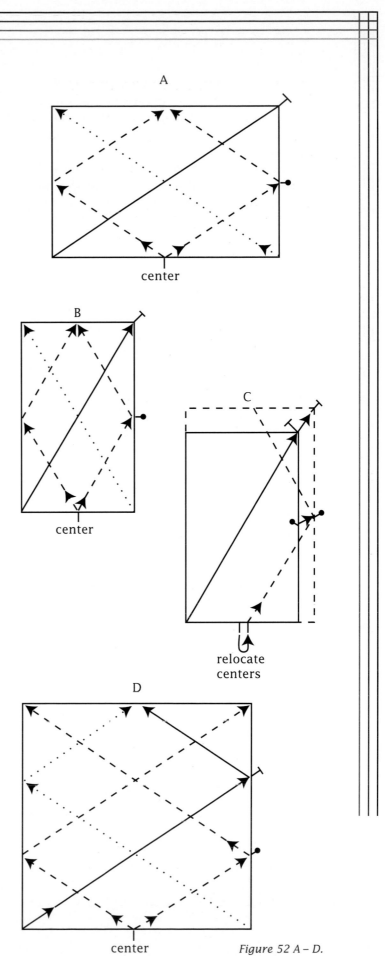

Figure 52 A – D.

CALCULATING THE ODD-ANGLE COMMENCEMENT EDGE

The relationship of strand width to length of commencement edge varies with the setting angle (Figure 53). A strand tilted less than the usual 45° requires less space along the edge than 1.42 times its width. A strand tilted more than 45° requires more space. There is a simple, practical way to find the length you need for the commencement edge – or the number of strands you need for the width of mat you want.

Along the edge of a paper lay 10 strands of the desired width and the intended angle. Mark and measure the space they take. Divide by 10. This is easier than trying to measure a tiny space accurately.

For example, if 10 strands take up 17", each strand requires 1.7". A 20 strand layout fills a 34" commencement edge. If 10 strands take up only 12", each requires 1.2" A 20-strand layout fills a 24" edge. *Remember to add expansion allowance to these.*

In Figure 52 side edges differ from commencement edges because strand angles differ. Once you've decided your design-to-shape relationship, you can repeat the calculation to find side lengths, if you need to know in advance.

HOW LONG IS A STRAND?

The simplest way to find out is to mark your underlay (Figure 52). Trace the course of one strand, allowing for possible expansion of the

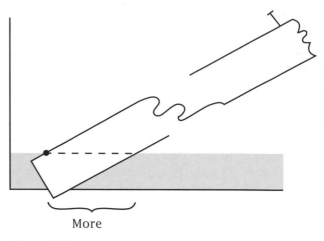

More

Figure 53 B.

mat. Add safety and finishing allowances as for any diagonal mat. If LP and RP are the same strand, double the result.

To encourage you, I worked mat C from Plate 150 in paper strips of four values. I used a steep angle similar to mat B in Figure 52, and enlivened it with twill. You can see how the angle affects these figures and the ala of LP over two, RP over two (Plate 154). Compare this with the same ala in standard diagonal set, in the photo instructions that follow.

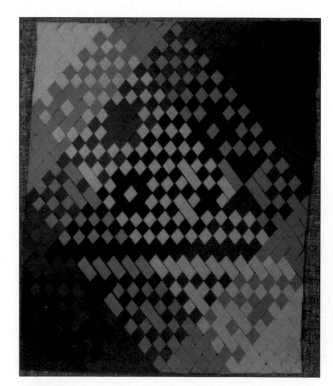

Plate 154.

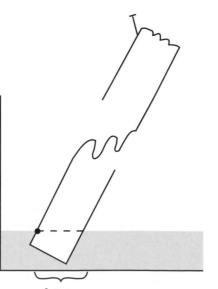

Less

Figure 53 A.

THE COMPLETE TWILL ALA

Twill repeat patterns are many, almost any combination of skips you can imagine. The order of working and hand movements become more complicated as more RP and LP are involved. These patterns are worked across the mat as one ala depth, as you did for the over three, over three twill.

Getting into twill at one edge of the mat and out at the other is the most difficult part. Begin at the left with checker, move into twill, and finish with checker at the right edge.

The photos and diagrams that follow show how to plait an ala of LP over two, RP over two. Prepare strips for a practice mat in corner start, RP and LP: 5D, 5L, 5D. Fold the commencement edge upward, left edge under, as usual. Work an ala of checkerwork as a foundation. Sweep back all LP except the first at the left.

Raise a new ala of two up and two down, as in Plate 155. The white RP at the edge has just been folded.

Do not open the row for checkerwork. Instead, raise RP 1 (in my right hand in Plate 156). Lower the LP across the three nearest RP, and under the raised one. This is an intermediate step that shows permanently in the mat as an LP stroke over three.

For the next working row (Plate 157) leave the *two* nearest RP down. Raise RP 2 and 3 together. Leave RP 1 behind.

Lay in the LP (Plate 158).

Lower RP 2 and 3, but immediately pair RP 3 with RP 4. Leave RP 2 behind. Raise RP 3 and 4

Plate 156.

Plate 157.

Plate 155.

Plate 158.

121

Plate 159.

together (Plate 159). This opens the next working row for LP "over two, under two."

Lay in the next LP. Lower the two RP (Plate 160). Drop RP 3 and pick up RP 5 with RP 4. You can see the RP strokes over two LP form one at a time as you do this.

Continue the ala in this manner, picking up one RP to the right as you leave one behind at the left. The order of working is: raise two RP together, lay in one LP, lower two RP, drop one to the left, pick up one more to the right.

When you reach the right-hand edge of the mat you will run out of LP. Plate 161 shows the ala and your position. You are lowering two RP, with three more remaining at right.

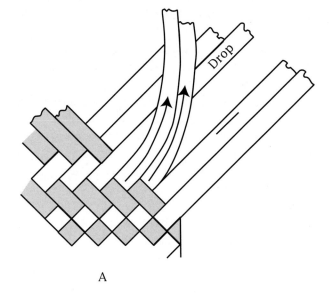

A

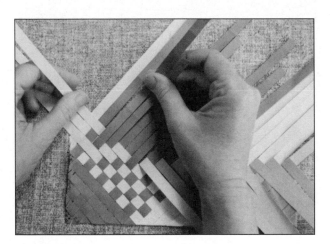

Plate 160.

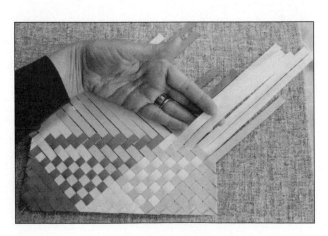

Plate 161.

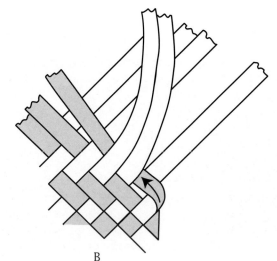

B

Figure 54 A – B.

122

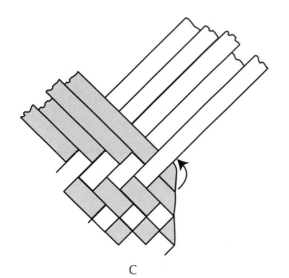

C

Figure 54 C.

Plate 162.

To complete the right-hand edge follow Figures 54 A – C.

A. Drop the RP at left and pick up on the right. This leaves two RP free at the edge.

B. Fold the edge RP (farthest to right) upward and to the left. Lay this new LP into the row, under the two raised RP.

C. Lower the two RP. Fold the remaining RP at the edge *under* and to the left. Take it behind only the *one* (nearest) RP. This restores checkerwork in this last stroke of the ala. As the next ala reaches the edge, RP will fold upward as usual.

Sweep back LP and return to the left edge for the next ala.

TUBE STRAND MATS AS GARMENTS:
A SIMPLE ADAPTATION

The LP over two, RP over two twill ala provides pattern emphasis at the hipline of the "Weaver Wizards" wrap skirt. As I mentioned earlier, tightening the holding cord after weaving shapes the waistline. This is my basic recipe. Alter the ingredients to your own taste. The skirt fits up to 26" waist, 36" hip. To enlarge, add more strands at the commencement edge. With a small front overlap, the skirt is worn over tights or shorts (Plate 162).

Fabric: 4 yards unbleached muslin or plain white cotton, washed several times to remove sizing. Cut into two lengths of two yards. Paint each with a different wash of fiber-reactive dye. (I used Procion MX yellow, fuchsia, and blue,

blended to make orange and purple as well.) Change hues quickly at the center of each length, where RP fold to become LP. Alternately, buy hand-dyed fabric.

Strands: 56 tube strands, ½" finished width, 72" cut length, turned through openings in their sides and hand-stitched closed. 28 strands cut from each dyed fabric length.

Holding cord: dyed, 50" long for 41" commencement edge, plus ends for handling.

Set-up and layout: Physical set-up as for rag rug. Alternating sets of strands from each dye set, with centers slightly offset at the commencement to smear the color changes of LP and RP ends.

Lalanga pattern: Interlace, then checkerwork to a depth of 3" from the commencement edge.

•One ala of LP over two, RP over two twill.

•Checkerwork to 9" from the commencement edge.

•Repeat the twill ala. (I used a more difficult combination, with *no more than two skips* at a time.)

•Checkerwork to 20", or depth desired, from commencement edge, remainder as fringe.

STABILIZATION AND EMBELLISHMENT:

Left edge: Tie every strand intersection with a double strand of pearl cotton #8. For positioning see A in Figure 55 (page 124).

Right edge: This is the wrap-over edge. Tie every strand intersection with two or three strands of pearl cotton #8. Into some of them incorporate more pearl cotton and glitter braid. Mix hues and shades to enhance the immediate area. (Review technique in Figure 8.) Trim to about 2" for irregular shag fringe down the edge.

Final edge fringe: Tie every strand intersection with two or three strands of pearl cotton, making a visible cross-stitch on the back. For positioning see B in Figure 55. Add glitter braid every third intersection or so. Trim 3" – 4" length.

Waist: Draw up the cord until the skirt rests on the hipbone. Distribute fullness and hand stitch the ends of the commencement edge to the cord. Stitch in several places along the edge. Knot the cord close to the end stitching. Lead its loose ends back through the edge. Sew skirt hooks at waist and hip along the overlap, concealed by the edge. Fit the bars (eyes) to the wearer. Velcro is also a possibility.

Figure 55 suggests locations for embellishing and stabilizing stitches on twill figures and edges of tube strand mats. Some of these appear on Lanu Lalanga (Plate 151).

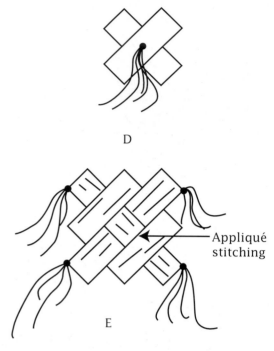

Appliqué stitching

Figure 55 D – E.

FLYING TIME – REVERSE THINKING

What if you weave a corner-start diagonal mat with double-faced strands – solid color on one side, print on the other? As you fold strands at the edges, what happens to the fall of prints and solids? How would the effect of strands with sharply contrasting faces differ from the effect of little contrast between print and solid faces?

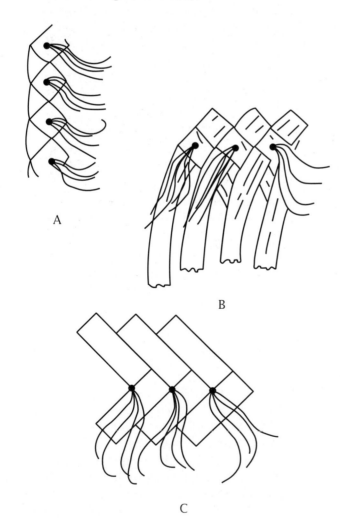

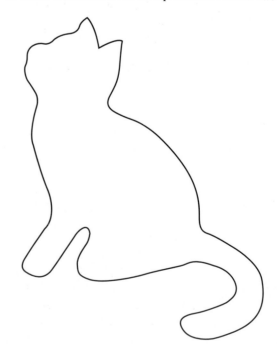

Figure 55 A – C.

124

Plate 163. "Weaverthink," 52" x 52". ©1993 Shari Cole . A pieced quilt designed by plaiting paper strip. See "A Digression" in Chapter 7 for notes on piecing from plaited models. To sharpen the ray of light effect, I substituted bright yellow for gold in the first two strands laid at the commencement corner. Some twill figures are contained within a given checkerboard "block." Others spill across color boundaries. Machine quilting in the ditch with invisible nylon thread on top imitates the natural contour of plaited surfaces.

Chapter Eleven

Widening the Weaver's Path

In Chapter 6 we looked at the effects of different strand widths on the shapes of curved plaiting (Figure 16). If crossing strands of equal widths makes squares, crossing strands of different widths will make rectangles. Polynesian weavers use this idea in handbags and hampers, often with narrow verticals in one value and wider horizontals in another value. How can we extend this idea in fabric design?

CONTROLLED EXPERIMENTS
WITH STRAND WIDTHS

Let's go beyond simple differences between horizontals and verticals and examine more complicated strategies in checkerwork. I have organized these from most to least ordered, and plaited samples in paper.

So that we compare the same thing from one sample to the next, my basic unit is 1/8". Increases and decreases are counted in that unit using 13 widths: 1/8, 2/8 (1/4), 3/8, 4/8 (1/2), 5/8, 6/8 (3/4), 7/8, 8/8 (1), 9/8, (1 1/8) 10/8 (1 1/4), 11/8, (1 3/8) 12/8 (1 1/2), and 13/8. (1 5/8) This small unit is convenient for exploration and translates well into ribbon weaving. For fabric strands use 1/4" or 1/2" instead.

Two contrasting values, light Vrt and dark Hrz, give maximum effect. Follow the outline below, a selection from among the many possible variables.

I. Horizontal Weave:

A. Vrt all the same width, Hrz of varied widths. (Since the initial width of Vrt influences the effect, samples have two sections. One section uses narrow 2/8" strands, the other 6/8" strands as Vrt.)

1. Regular changes in Hrz widths. Follow these in Plates 164 and 165, following. View them vertically and sideways.

a. From bottom to top – 1/8" to 12/8"

b. From bottom to top and back again – 9/8" to 1/8" decrease to center. How would increase look?

c. Increase – decrease repeated as a wave:

(1) Six steps, 1/8" to 6/8". With larger units the effect is reduced as the *percentage* of change is reduced so instead try...

(2) The first six steps of the Fibonacci series – 1, 2, 3, 5, 8, 13. Often seen in bargello embroidery and strip piecing, this series appears in nature, for example, the increase in the chamber size of spiral seashells.

2. Random changes in width of Hrz.

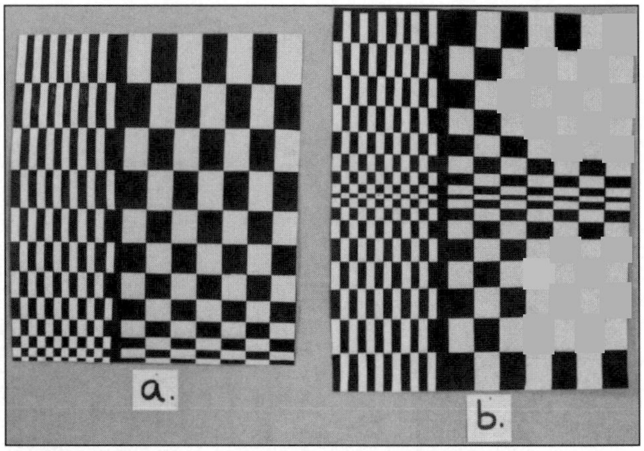

Plate 164.

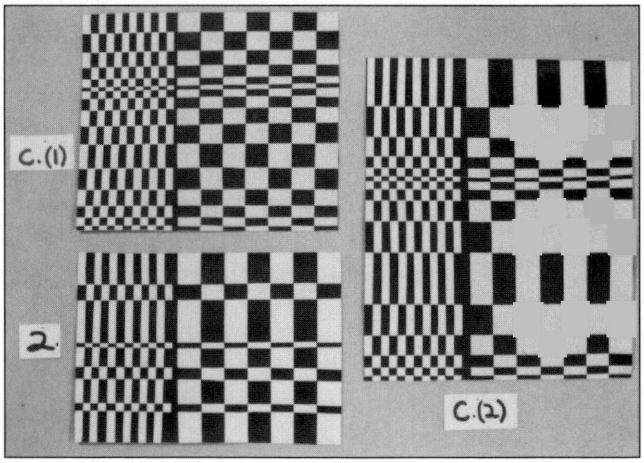

Plate 165.

Now join me as the game escalates. Plait your own samples and compare them to those below. Use more or fewer strands if you like. View them horizontally and on point, near and far away.

B. Both Vrt and Hrz change width:

1. Regular change, both sets at the same rate.

a. From first strand in to last strand in,

counting from lower-left corner. See Plate 65 (Chapter 5) for *decrease* 12⁄8" to 1⁄8".

b. From edges to center and back again. A decrease of 8⁄8" to 1⁄8" is shown as b. (1) in Plate 166, the Fibonacci series b. (2). In Plate 16 (Chapter 1) you see a gradual metric increase.

c. One set decreases to center; the other set increases. See c in Plate 163 for 1⁄8" to 8⁄8" change. How is this related to Plate 65?

d. Increase – decrease repeated as a wave from first strand in (d in Plate 166), with 1⁄8" to 6⁄8". Compare to A.1.c in Plate 165.

2. Random changes to both sets of strands. There is no example. Anything you produce is valid, but some will make better design starters than others.

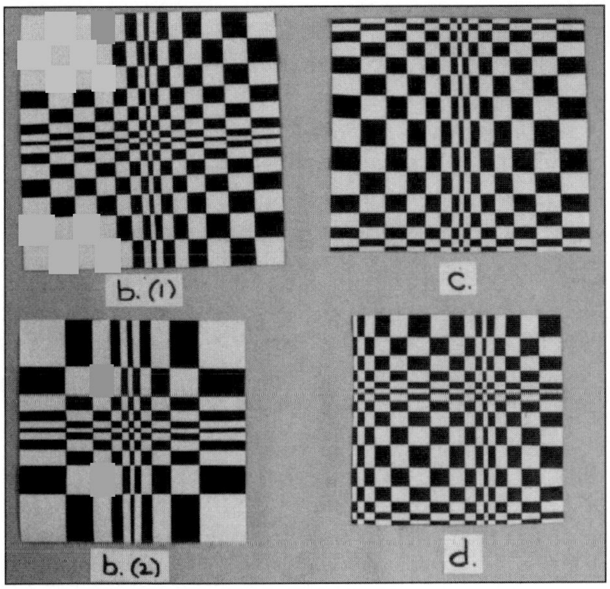

Plate 166.

Must strands be confined to the rectangle? What construction problems arise when you let cloth strands escape from the weave?

II. DIAGONAL WEAVE:

A few of my experiments appear in Plate 167.

A. Corner start – RP and LP the same strand, value *groups*.

1. Widest strand in first and decrease, 9⁄8" to 1⁄8". Layout pattern: 3L (9⁄8, 8⁄8, 7⁄8) 3D (6⁄8, 5⁄8, 4⁄8) 3L remainder.

2. Repeat 1 above, but increase again – 3L, 3D, 3L as above, then *2*L (2⁄8, 3⁄8) 3D, 3L = 17 strands total. (You won't believe your ala, but these irregular diagonal blocks do come out right in the end.)

3. Random widths in value groups of three.

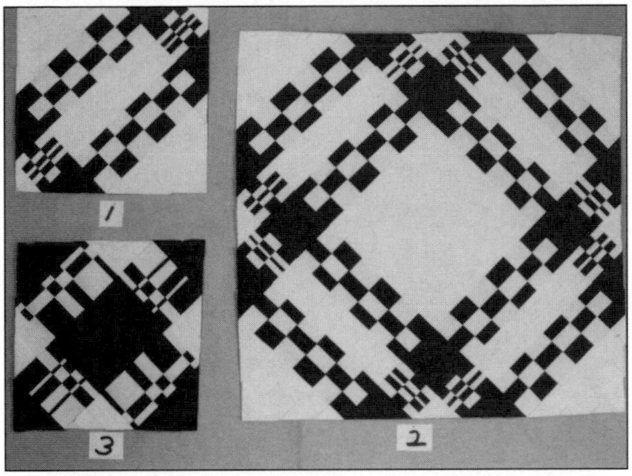

Plate 167.

I encourage you to extend this outline, asking for more variations. What happens? What do you have to do? What can you do with the results?

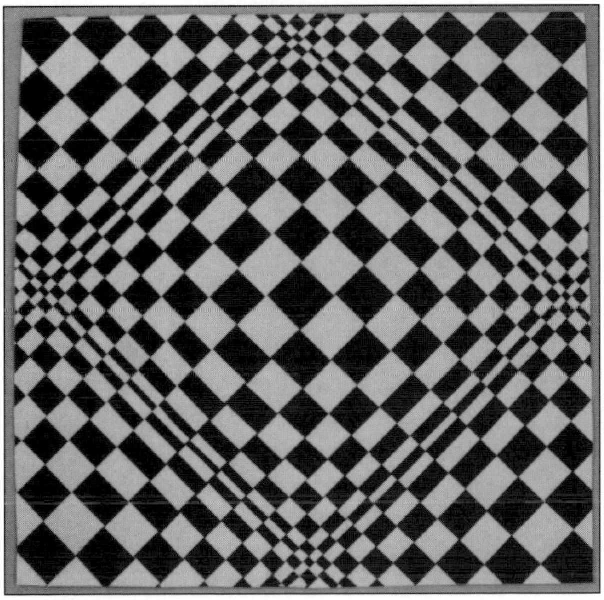

Plate 168.

Is the block in Plate 168 horizontal or diagonal weave? Where did I start? In the center of the block. How did I know where to stop? A square underlay told me. Add center start to your permutations.

Compare the samples above for illusions of depth and curve. Experiment with the rate of changes to width. Which blocks would enhance a garment? Which would create awkward effects? Might the awkward ones work well as small-scale accents, perhaps in ribbon?

Be aware that introducing one more value, or a second hue, will double the number of block variations. So will any change to strand widths, or to the number of strands. If the permutations here are not infinite, they are close enough to it for any quilter's lifetime.

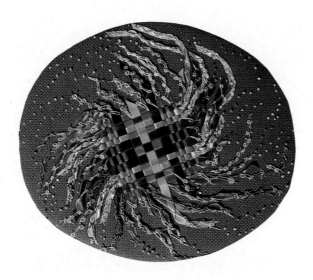

Plate 169.

ORDER INTO CHAOS

"Tinkerbell vs. the Establishment" contrasts orderly rectangles of plaited ribbons with the stardust flight of escaping ends (Plate 169). Fusible web holds the plaiting to aida embroidery cloth, while ends are supported by surface stitches in perle cotton and metallic braid. The stitches flow from a feeling of rotation. Are the ends really escaping, or do they propel the whole system through space?

CHAOS INTO ORDER: A BLOCK IMPROVEMENT PROJECT.

I'm with the Tinkerbells of the world when it comes to decking the geometric halls with flying ribbons, but a television set in my old-fashioned country living room is just *too* incongruent. I can't wave a magic wand and make it disappear, but I can drop a block quilt over it.

BLOCK QUILTS

What's a block quilt? It's a six block quilt made up as a cube instead of flat – or a box of five blocks if you don't need a bottom panel. Block quilts hide ugly things. They keep dust out of toasters and sewing machines. They soak up the condensation that drips from toilet tanks in the summer. Some people would call them "appliance covers," thus rendering them invisible. I call them Block Quilts and lavish as much care on their design and construction as I would if they were flat.

Our experiments with variable-width strands are perfect for my television-hiding block quilt. Television distorts reality, so I shall distort the black box in my living room. No graphic op-art for this autumn-toned room, but something low contrast and harmonious.

I will plait ironed-over edge strands on firm needlepunch and backing, one block each for front, back, top, and sides. I will remember to leave extra allowance on each block for easy removal, and in case the machine quilting shrinks the size more than expected. This television has no protruding leads at the back, but if it had, a bias-bound cut out would protect them. How will I join these blocks together?

I can sew them by machine, right sides together, and trim some of the needlepunch batting from the seam allowances after sewing each seam. To finish seams, I can zigzag stitch, pink, or bind raw edges. For this construction I sew all four sides to the top first, ending stitching at the seam line of corners, not at the edge of the fabric. I sew the four side seams last, from corner to bottom. It may be necessary to hand baste the corner end of the seam before stitching. Bias bind the bottom of the box.

BACK ART FOR DEPARTING QUILTERS

A good place for these plaited optical illusion blocks is on your back. People are used to seeing emblems on the backs of jackets and vests. Make your good impressions last – as you leave the room.

High contrast emphasizes the op-art effect. For subtlety choose less contrast, perhaps with prints included. You might flash narrow horizontals of bright colors across your shoulders to broaden them. Keep values darker and contrast lower in waist and hip areas. You can cover the whole back piece of the pattern with plaiting, or add just a block.

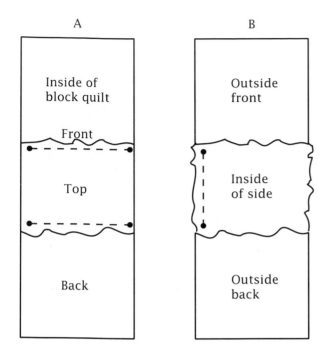

A

Inside of
block quilt

Front

Top

Back

B

Outside
front

Inside
of side

Outside
back

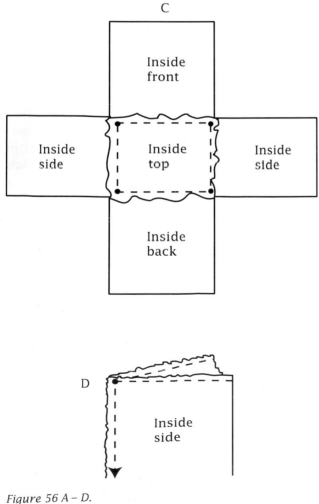

C

Inside
front

Inside
side

Inside
top

Inside
side

Inside
back

D

Inside
side

Figure 56 A – D.

APPLYING A PLAITED BLOCK TO A REVERSIBLE LINING

While the "Frog Printses" dress (Plate 131) has no plaited inserts, we can use the same fabric collage technique to apply them as I used to apply fabrics directly to the dress lining. Bias binding covers raw edges and unifies the many prints with its own subtle print texture.

1. Place the base (lining) fabric *wrong side up* on your weaving board. Trace the pattern piece, including seam allowance onto the fabric.

2. Apply fusible web to the area to be covered with plaiting, as for the purple blouse in Plate 67.

3. Plait your design on this area. If you use ironed-over edge strands, unfold the seam allowances of the outside strands, as for the plaited quilt blocks in Figure 10 (Chapter 6).

4. Fuse the plaiting. Trim strand ends to ¼".

5. Frame the plaiting with the fabric to appear on the right side of the rest of that pattern piece. Two methods follow in Figures 58 and 59.

6. Lay the paper pattern piece on the finished assembly. Retrace it on the surface.

7. Add any machine quilting or decorative stitching. *Then* pin the paper pattern in place and cut out the piece.

8. Assemble the garment. You can treat each piece as one layer, or conceal the inside seams. To do so, stitch garment pieces with *outside* layers together. Then fold the lining fabric seam allowance in on one side and hand stitch the seam (see Figure 57 A – C.).

Plaited panels, and the methods below of finishing the garment piece, work best on simple garment shapes. When choosing a pattern, and deciding how to fill the remaining space on the

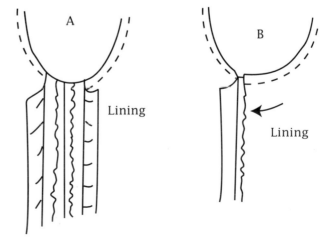

A

Lining

B

Lining

Figure 57 A – B.

Chapter Twelve
DIVERGING PATHS: STRANDS IN THE NET

We've come a long way with the Mothers of Invention, and I hope you've had a few A-ha's along the way. They let go of our hands several forks back and went off to invent other things. We didn't notice, because we were too busy chasing ideas up side tracks.

By now you realize that these paths and tracks are more like a net than a branching road system. When you ask for one new thing you have to make decisions about a lot of other things. Once you decide the form of a project – quilt, garment, art object – you can permute the possiblities of all the variables:

- Type of strand
- Width of strands
- Directional set of strands in the weave
- Values, hues, intensities of color
- Solid and print fabrics
- Checker and twill patterns
- Embellishments, appliqué, embroidery
- Designing pieced patchwork by weaving paper
- Wild cards

PLAYING PERMUTATIONS
FOR ALL THEY'RE WORTH

Which forms of these variables have we worked with? How many others will you invent? You don't know how much you know until you look at your work and remember all the decisions that went into it.

Let's outline just one set of permutations, organizing them from the obvious and ordered to the risky and chaotic. Value layout strategies are central to our designs. They are listed here as they apply to *diagonal weave only,* with some examples given.

VALUE LAYOUT STRATEGIES – DIAGONAL WEAVE
I. With LP and RP as the same strand
   A. *Groups* of same-value strands
      1. Arranged symmetrically from the center of the commencement edge ("Rag Rug Ramble," Plate 148).
      2. Corners the same value group, but group order mixed along the commencement edge (Plate 150, mat A Chapter 9).

3. Value groups arranged from one corner to the other in arbitrary order (Plate 150, mat B).
4. Value groups shaded light to dark, from one corner to the other (Plate 150, mat C).
5. Individual strands of two groups intercut (Plate 172). Intercutting the light and dark strands of mat C opens a whole new line of inquiry.

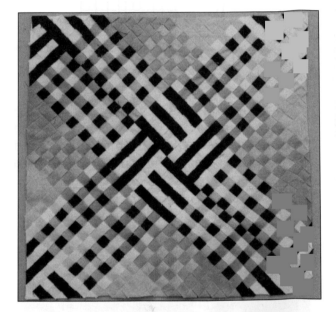

Plate 172.

B. Some strands grouped, others laid in as individual strands:
   1. Shaded from light to dark
   2. Laid in as a planned repeat
   3. Laid in randomly

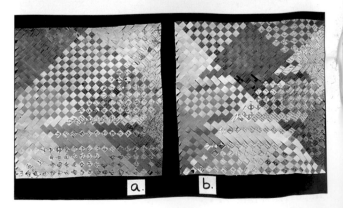

Plate 173.

132

II. With double-faced strands so LP and RP separate themselves into two fabrics – for example, plain and print – upon rebounding from the edge.

•Strategies above apply. "Weaverthink" (Plate 163) is Strategy A.3.

III. With single-sided strands or single-fabric tubes, set separately as RP and LP at the commencement edge.

•Strategies above apply to *sets of RP* and to *sets of LP* independently.

For example, in Plate 173 *both* mats employ 20 RP in scribble prints arranged from left lower corner to right lower corner in groups of 3 very light, 7 light, 7 light medium, 3 medium. *Mat A* employs LP in groups of solids, from left to right as 3 very light, 7 light, 7 light medium, 3 medium. *Mat B* reverses the LP groups – medium, light medium, light, very light. What a difference one small change makes in the fall of light and the resulting composition. Both mats are Strategy A.4.

Both paper mats were trials for the layout of our permutation quilt in Chapter 10. I chose mat A as better for showing off twill. I kept mat B for another day. The quilt itself is Strategy B.1, print RP shaded individually, solid LP grouped by value.

Weaving Your Own Way

If you thrive on organization and planning, you can outline all the permutations in the book. You can chart the variables above and plan projects from the chart. Some combinations don't work well, but you find out by trying. If the path you take ends in a swamp, go back to the fork and choose another.

But if detail and paperwork bog you down, just make decisions as you go. Island weavers think ahead, but don't analyze and agonize. Experience guides them. Because you have more choices, you need more experience.

Weaving with the Fates

Many indigenous craftspeople take an attitude of reverence toward their work. Because they process the materials from their source in nature they feel the connection between life force and object. Their own thoughts and intentions are part of this concept as they construct the object. We have something of the same attitude when we speak of "quilts made with love."

Plate 174.

I find this works two ways. What you see, hear, and think while weaving and stitching, you remember later when seeing that pattern. Make your work place as pleasant and serene as possible. Let your hands dance to the music you love, to wind and birdsong, to conversations with friends and family. Weave joy into your work, and draw joy from it again.

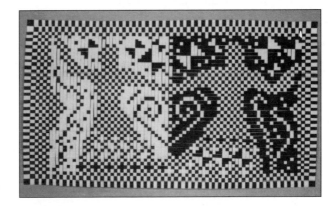

Plate 175.

133

BIBLIOGRAPHY

The following books are useful in exploring the ideas we have discussed, and open other avenues to you as well.

Plaiting and Polynesian Design Applied to Fabric
Arbeit, Wendy. *What Are Fronds For?* Honolulu, HI: University of Hawaii Press, 1985.
Cole, Shari. *Pacific Patchworks, New Approaches to Quilt Design.* Auckland, New Zealand: Pitman Craft Series, Longman Paul, 1988. Distributed in North America by University of Hawaii Press, Honolulu.
Robertson, Ailsa. *Patterns of Polynesia – Samoa.* Heinemann Education, Auckland: Octopus Publishing Group, Ltd. (NZ), 1989.
Pendergrast, Mick. *Feathers and Fibre, A Survey of Traditional and Contemporary Maori Craft.* Auckland, New Zealand: Penguin Books, Ltd, 1984.

Using Color and Fabric Prints in Quiltmaking
Beyer, Jinny. *Color Confidence for Quilters.* San Francisco, CA: The Quilt Digest Press, 1992.
Penders, Mary Coyne. *Color and Cloth.* San Francisco, CA: The Quilt Digest Press, 1989.
Wolfrom, Joen. *Magical Effects of Color.* Layfayette, CA: C & T Publishing, 1992.

South Pacific Bedcovers and Their Place in the Makers' Lives
Hammond, Joyce D. *Tifaifai and Quilts of Polynesia.* Honolulu, HI: University of Hawaii Press, 1986.
Rongokea, Lynnsay. *Tivaevae, Portraits of Cook Islands Quilting.* Wellington, New Zealand: Daphne Brasell Associates Press, Thorndon, 1992.

Seminole Patchwork
Rush, Beverly and Lassie Wittman. *The Complete Book of Seminole Patchwork: From Traditional Methods to Contemporary Uses.* Seattle: Madrona, 1982.

Each of these books in turn lists other useful books.

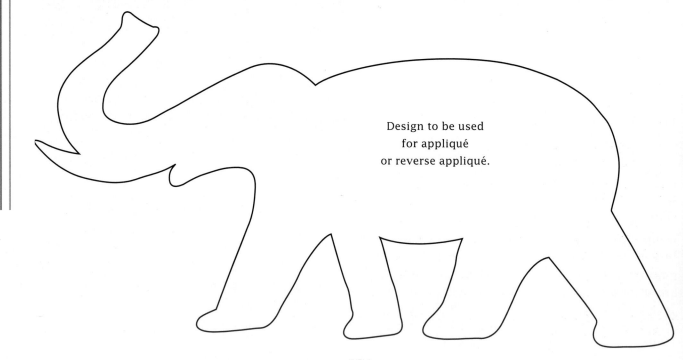

Design to be used
for appliqué
or reverse appliqué.

~American Quilter's Society~

dedicated to publishing books for today's quilters

The following AQS publications are currently available:

- **Adapting Architectural Details for Quilts,** Carol Wagner, #2282: AQS, 1992, 88 pages, softbound, $12.95

- **American Beauties: Rose & Tulip Quilts,** Gwen Marston & Joe Cunningham, #1907: AQS, 1988, 96 pages, softbound, $14.95

- **American Quilt Blocks: 50 Patterns for 50 States,** Beth Summers, #4543: AQS, 1995 ,168 pages, softbound, $16.95

- **Appliqué Designs: My Mother Taught Me to Sew,** Faye Anderson, #2121: AQS, 1990, 80 pages, softbound, $12.95

- **Appliqué Patterns from Native American Beadwork Designs,** Dr. Joyce Mori, #3790: AQS, 1994, 96 pages, softbound, $14.95

- **The Art of Hand Appliqué,** Laura Lee Fritz, #2122: AQS, 1990, 80 pages, softbound, $14.95

- **...Ask Helen More About Quilting Designs,** Helen Squire, #2099: AQS, 1990, 54 pages, 17 x 11, spiral-bound, $14.95

- **Award-Winning Quilts & Their Makers, Vol. I: The Best of AQS Shows – 1985-1987,** #2207: AQS, 1991, 232 pages, softbound, $24.95

- **Award-Winning Quilts & Their Makers, Vol. II: The Best of AQS Shows – 1988-1989,** #2354: AQS, 1992, 176 pages, softbound, $24.95

- **Award-Winning Quilts & Their Makers, Vol. III: The Best of AQS Shows – 1990-1991,** #3425: AQS, 1993, 180 pages, softbound, $24.95

- **Award-Winning Quilts & Their Makers, Vol. IV: The Best of AQS Shows – 1992-1993,** #3791: AQS, 1994, 180 pages, softbound, $24.95

- **Celtic Style Floral Appliqué: Designs Using Interlaced Scrollwork,** Scarlett Rose, #3926: AQS, 1995, 128 pages, softbound, $14.95

- **Classic Basket Quilts,** Elizabeth Porter & Marianne Fons, #2208: AQS, 1991, 128 pages, softbound, $16.95

- **A Collection of Favorite Quilts,** Judy Florence, #2119: AQS, 1990, 136 pages, softbound, $18.95

- **Creative Machine Art,** Sharee Dawn Roberts, #2355: AQS, 1992, 142 pages, 9 x 9, softbound, $24.95

- **Dear Helen, Can You Tell Me?...All About Quilting Designs,** Helen Squire, #1820: AQS, 1987, 51 pages, 17 x 11, spiral-bound, $12.95

- **Double Wedding Ring Quilts: New Quilts from an Old Favorite,** #3870: AQS, 1994, 112 pages, softbound, $14.95

- **Dye Painting!,** Ann Johnston, #3399: AQS, 1992, 88 pages, softbound, $19.95

- **Dyeing & Overdyeing of Cotton Fabrics,** Judy Mercer Tescher, #2030: AQS, 1990, 54 pages, softbound, $9.95

- **Encyclopedia of Pieced Quilt Patterns,** compiled by Barbara Brackman, #3468: AQS, 1993, 552 pages, hardbound, $34.95

- **Fabric Postcards: Landmarks & Landscapes • Monuments & Meadows,** Judi Warren, #3846: AQS, 1994, 120 pages, softbound, $22.95

- **Flavor Quilts for Kids to Make: Complete Instructions for Teaching Children to Dye, Decorate & Sew Quilts,** Jennifer Amor, #2356: AQS, 1991, 120 pages, softbound, $12.95

- **From Basics to Binding: A Complete Guide to Making Quilts,** Karen Kay Buckley, #2381: AQS, 1992, 160 pages, softbound, $16.95

- **Fun & Fancy Machine Quiltmaking,** Lois Smith, #1982: AQS, 1989, 144 pages, softbound, $19.95

- **Gatherings: America's Quilt Heritage,** Kathlyn F. Sullivan, #4526: AQS, 1995, 224 pages, 10 x 8½, softbound, $34.95

- **Heirloom Miniatures,** Tina M. Gravatt, #2097: AQS, 1990, 64 pages, softbound, $9.95

- **Infinite Stars,** Gayle Bong, #2283: AQS, 1992, 72 pages, softbound, $12.95

- **The Ins and Outs: Perfecting the Quilting Stitch,** Patricia J. Morris, #2120: AQS, 1990, 96 pages, softbound, $9.95

- **Irish Chain Quilts: A Workbook of Irish Chains & Related Patterns,** Joyce B. Peaden, #1906: AQS, 1988, 96 pages, softbound, $14.95

- **Jacobean Appliqué: Book I, "Exotica,"** Patricia B. Campbell & Mimi Ayars, Ph.D, #3784: AQS, 1993, 160 pages, softbound, $18.95

- **Jacobean Appliqué: Book II, "Romantica,"** Patricia B. Campbell & Mimi Ayars, Ph.D, #4544: AQS, 1995, 160 pages, softbound, $18.95

- **The Judge's Task: How Award-Winning Quilts Are Selected,** Patricia J. Morris, #3904: AQS, 1993, 128 pages, softbound, $19.95

- **Log Cabin Quilts: New Quilts from an Old Favorite,** edited by Victoria Faoro, #4523: AQS, 1995, 128 pages, softbound, $14.95

- **Marbling Fabrics for Quilts: A Guide for Learning & Teaching,** Kathy Fawcett & Carol Shoaf, #2206: AQS, 1991, 72 pages, softbound, $12.95

- **Mola Techniques for Today's Quilters,** Charlotte Patera, #4514: AQS, 1995, 112 pages, softbound, $18.95

- **More Projects and Patterns: A Second Collection of Favorite Quilts,** Judy Florence, #3330: AQS, 1992, 152 pages, softbound, $18.95

- **Nancy Crow: Quilts and Influences,** Nancy Crow, #1981: AQS, 1990, 256 pages, 9 x 12, hardcover, $29.95

(Continued)

- **Nancy Crow: Work in Transition,** Nancy Crow, #3331: AQS, 1992, 32 pages, 9 x 10, softbound, $12.95

- **New Jersey Quilts – 1777 to 1950: Contributions to an American Tradition,** The Heritage Quilt Project of New Jersey; text by Rachel Cochran, Rita Erickson, Natalie Hart & Barbara Schaffer, #3332: AQS, 1992, 256 pages, softbound, $29.95

- **New Patterns from Old Architecture,** Carol Wagner, #3927: AQS, 1995, 72 pages, softbound, $12.95

- **No Dragons on My Quilt,** Jean Ray Laury with Ritva Laury & Lizabeth Laury, #2153: AQS, 1990, 52 pages, hardcover, $12.95

- **Old Favorites in Miniature,** Tina Gravatt, #3469: AQS, 1993, 104 pages, softbound, $15.95

- **Paint and Patches: Painting on Fabrics with Pigment,** Vicki L. Johnson, #4515: AQS, 1995, 144 pages, softbound, $18.95

- **A Patchwork of Pieces: An Anthology of Early Quilt Stories 1845-1940,** complied by Cuesta Ray Benberry and Carol Pinney Crabb, #3333: AQS, 1993, 360 pages, 5½ x 8½, softbound, $14.95

- **Precision Patchwork for Scrap Quilts, Anytime, Anywhere...,** Jeannette Muir, #3928: AQS, 1995, 72 pages, softbound, $12.95

- **Quilt Groups Today: Who They Are, Where They Meet, What They Do, and How to Contact Them – A Complete Guide for 1992-1993,** #3308: AQS, 1992, 336 pages, softbound, $14.95

- **A Quilted Christmas,** edited by Bonnie Browning, #4542: AQS, 1995, 160 pages, softbound, $18.95

- **Quilter's Registry,** Lynne Fritz, #2380: AQS, 1992, 80 pages, 5½ x 8½, hardbound, $9.95

- **Quilting Patterns from Native American Designs,** Dr. Joyce Mori, #3467: AQS, 1993, 80 pages, softbound, $12.95

- **Quilting With Style: Principles for Great Pattern Design,** Gwen Marston & Joe Cunningham, #3470: AQS, 1993, 192 pages, hardbound, $24.95

- **Quiltmaker's Guide: Basics & Beyond,** Carol Doak, #2284: AQS, 1992, 208 pages, softbound, $19.95

- **Quilts: The Permanent Collection – MAQS,** #2257: AQS, 1991, 100 pages, 10 x 6½, softbound, $9.95

- **Quilts: The Permanent Collection – MAQS, Volume II,** #3793: AQS, 1994, 80 pages, 10 x 6½, softbound, $9.95

- **Roots, Feathers & Blooms: 4-Block Quilts, Their History & Patterns, Book I,** Linda Giesler Carlson, #3789: AQS, 1994, 128 pages, softbound, $16.95

- **Sampler Quilt Blocks from Native American Designs,** Dr. Joyce Mori, #4512: AQS, 1995, 80 pages, softbound, $14.95

- **Seasons of the Heart & Home: Quilts for a Winter's Day,** Jan Patek, #3796: AQS, 1993, 160 pages, softbound, $18.95

- **Seasons of the Heart & Home: Quilts for Summer Days,** Jan Patek, #3761: AQS, 1993, 160 pages, softbound, $18.95

- **Sensational Scrap Quilts,** Darra Duffy Williamson, #2357: AQS, 1992, 152 pages, softbound, $24.95

- **Show Me Helen...How to Use Quilting Designs,** Helen Squire, #3375: AQS, 1993, 155 pages, softbound, $15.95

- **Somewhere in Between: Quilts and Quilters of Illinois,** Rita Barrow Barber, #1790: AQS, 1986, 78 pages, softbound, $14.95

- **Spike & Zola: Patterns for Laughter...and Appliqué, Painting, or Stenciling,** Donna French Collins, #3794: AQS, 1993, 72 pages, softbound, $9.95

- **The Stori Book of Embellishing: Great Ideas for Quilts and Garments,** Mary Stori, #3929: AQS, 1994, 96 pages, softbound, $16.95

- **Straight Stitch Machine Appliqué: History, Patterns & Instructions for This Easy Technique,** Letty Martin, #3903: AQS, 1994, 160 pages, softbound, $16.95

- **Striplate Piecing: Piecing Circle Designs with Speed and Accuracy,** Debra Wagner, #3792: AQS, 1994, 168 pages 9 x 12, hardbound, $24.95

- **Tessellations and Variations: Creating One-Patch & Two-Patch Quilts,** Barbara Ann Caron, #3930: AQS, 1994, 120 pages, softbound, $14.95

- **Three-Dimensional Appliqué and Embroidery Embellishment: Techniques for Today's Album Quilt,** Anita Shackelford, #3788: AQS, 1993, 152 pages, 9 x 12, hardbound, $24.95

- **Time-Span Quilts: New Quilts from Old Tops,** Becky Herdle, #3931: AQS, 1994, 136 pages, softbound, $16.95

- **A Treasury of Quilting Designs,** Linda Goodmon Emery, #2029: AQS, 1990, 80 pages, 14 x 11, spiral-bound, $14.95

- **Tricks with Chintz: Using Large Prints to Add New Magic to Traditional Quilt Blocks,** Nancy S. Breland, #3847: AQS, 1994, 96 pages, softbound, $14.95

- **Wonderful Wearables: A Celebration of Creative Clothing,** Virginia Avery, #2286: AQS, 1991, 184 pages, softbound, $24.95

These books can be found in local bookstores and quilt shops. If you are unable to locate a title in your area, you can order by mail from AQS, P.O. Box 3290, Paducah, KY 42002-3290. Please add $2 for the first book and 40¢ for each additional one to cover postage and handling. (International orders please add $2.50 for the first book and $1 for each additional one.)